W9-BKR-155

THE COLLEGE PRESIDENCY:
Initiation into the Order of the Turtle

LB
2331.7
.R5

THE
College Presidency:
Initiation into the
Order of the Turtle

by

M. A. F. RITCHIE

LIBRARY

PHILOSOPHICAL LIBRARY
New York

Copyright, 1970, by PHILOSOPHICAL LIBRARY, INC.
15 East 40 Street, New York, N. Y. 10016

Library of Congress Catalog Card No. 70-100582

SBN 8022-2326-5

All rights reserved

MANUFACTURED IN THE UNITED STATES OF AMERICA

To Josephine

Who Has Stood
With Me All
the Way

AND

TO OUR CHILDREN

John, Jo Ann and Betsy

WHO HAVE SHARED
THESE EXPERIENCES

Foreword

College president M. A. F. Ritchie's book is the professional memoir of a creative and courageous leader, written at a time when the author had enough successful experience to write with authority and knowledge, and enough constructive years ahead of him to continue to use his knowledge.

It is recommended reading for the thoughtful leaders of the black community, especially the black educators.

It is recommended reading for the faculty who might well ponder the forthright statements on "tenure." Perhaps it points the way to modifying "tenure" so that it continues to protect that which is precious while there is still time.

It is almost required reading for those "strange bedfellows," trustees and regents, who give part of their time to do what has to be done.

President Ritchie's book is a constructive addition to the literature concerning the on-going, ever-changing, challenging job of assisting youth in the growing-up process, while at the same time protecting and enhancing the unique institution which appeals to many as the best place to be during these formative years.

REED O. HUNT
chairman of the Executive Committee, formerly chairman of the Board of Directors, Crown Zellerbach Corporation; trustee, Pacific University and California Institute of Technology; chairman of the Board of Regents of the University of San Francisco.

San Francisco
September 1, 1969

vii

TABLE OF CONTENTS

Preface

On my office desk there is a small brass turtle. Sometimes in a difficult conference I will find myself reaching for the small object. At other times I may do the same thing while making a difficult decision quite alone.

In either case I am reminding myself of the words inscribed on the inside back of the turtle:

> *"One cannot move ahead, or make progress*
> *without sticking out one's neck."*

The little turtle on my desk was sent me by Mrs. J. Roscoe Lee, Forest Grove, Oregon, at a time when I had my neck way out and was the subject of considerable criticism. In her note accompanying the gift she invited me to accept membership in the "Order of the Turtle." Even a person of Mrs. Lee's imagination and dedication could not possibly realize how much the sturdy little turtle has meant to me in trying to meet the tests of what has become the toughest educational job there is, the small college presidency.

Whatever may be the shortcomings of the American college president today, he can claim one distinction: Membership in the Order of the Turtle. To move his college forward, to initiate progress, he surely must stick out his neck. It is hoped that the book will contribute to a better understanding of a uniquely difficult and uniquely satisfying job.

Of course the book could not have been written without the help of many people. I am especially grateful to Ellis Lucia, noted for his books on the Northwest, for reading the manuscript critically. The James A. and Jessie Smith Dewar Foundation of Oneonta, New York, has supported this project with a generous grant for which I am deeply grateful. My secretaries, Mrs. Clara Beard and Mrs. Ruth Langton, and student office assistant Nancy Weber can never be repaid for their painstaking work. And if it had not been for the assistance and encouragement of my wife, Josephine, the project would still be unfinished.

M. A. F. RITCHIE

Pacific University
Forest Grove, Oregon
September 1, 1969

CHAPTER I

On Becoming a College President

The choice of college presidents perhaps could claim the dubious honor of being the most unscientific process in American life. Logan Wilson, president of the American Council on Education, has said: "Indeed, considering how college and university presidents are actually selected, it may be a cause for some astonishment that they are on the whole as able a category of leaders as can be found in any major occupational class."[1]

Certainly my becoming a college president in 1953 appeared to violate most, if not all, the premises of scientific planning. I had recently become a department head and a full professor in a growing, exciting university. I had no expectation whatever of leaving. And I had never heard of the college in question.

The story began with an unimportant looking letter in my mail at the University of Miami in June, 1952. The letter was addressed to Professor Ritchie, Human Relations Dept., University of Miami, Coral Gables, Florida. No first name, and no initials. As I opened it I thought perhaps it was from a late-applying school teacher wishing to attend my workshop in Intergroup Relations for the summer session.

Glancing through the letter hastily, I realized how wrong my assumption was. It was from a Mrs. Bertus C. Lauren, Oneonta, N. Y., who stated that she was a member of a committee to select a new president for Hartwick College to succeed Dr. Henry J. Arnold who would retire the following June, and it asked quite directly whether I would be interested in the job.

---

[1] *How College Presidents Are Chosen* by Frederick de W. Bolman, American Council on Education, Washington, D.C., 1965. Pg. v.

Mrs. Lauren also stated that she had heard of my career through my cousin, Dr. Chrisenberry A. Ritchie, Binghamton, N. Y., a member of Hartwick's Board of Trustees. The mention of his name brought back to mind that some thirty years before, this half-nephew of my father had visited our home in Churchville, Va. He had been for many years a prominent minister in upstate New York and had recently retired. Of course, I had no reason to believe that he even remembered me after so many years. Yet, apparently he had followed my career through the alumni magazine of Roanoke College from which both of us had been graduated.

That evening I took the letter home to my wife Josephine. She looked it over in some perplexity and then expressed my thought exactly by saying: "But what of your work here in developing a center for human relations studies?" Yet the two of us felt sort of "peculiar" about this letter which had come "entirely out of the blue." We decided I should at least give a courteous reply and express willingness to explore the matter without obligation. I wrote Mrs. Lauren to that effect.

I also wrote my cousin, Dr. Chrisenberry Ritchie, asking him about the situation. He replied in a very friendly letter indicating that he had suggested to the committee that they might wish to look into my qualifications. He made it plain that he wished the matter to be kept on a completely impersonal basis and that neither the committee nor I should be influenced by our being related.

Several weeks passed and I had no reply from Mrs. Lauren, so I turned my attention to other things. Then one day Dr. Charles Doren Tharp, Dean of the College of Arts and Sciences, hailed me with the question, "What's this I hear about your going north to be a college president?" My laughing rejoinder was, "Not much chance. I have apparently scared them off. But how did you know about it?"

Then Doren told me that he was receiving inquiries from New York by persons who obviously were doing an "academic gumshoe job" on me. This gave me great concern, and I left his office knowing that something serious was afoot.

During the months that followed we had a visit from Dr.

2

Arthur Seybolt, a member of the Board of Trustees of Hartwick College, then vacationing in St. Petersburg, Fla. He visited in our home and had lunch with us in Miami. I recall his saying, "What we need is a businessman at Hartwick College as president." And my reply, "Dr. Seybolt, I am not a businessman and therefore, in your view, I would certainly not be a good president." Of course, in addition, I made it plain to him that I had every appreciation for the point of view and experience of businessmen.

Apparently Dr. Seybolt's report was favorable since my next contact from the Board of Trustees was in the form of an invitation to come to Oneonta during the Christmas vacation. I was unable to accept due to other commitments during that period, but I agreed to meet with the Trustees in Albany on the 31st of January in an exploratory session.

It is doubtful whether I actually would have taken the trip to Albany had it not been for a long distance telephone call from Dr. Carroll V. Newsom, associate commissioner for Higher Education in the New York State Department of Education. He was very convincing. He captured my interest by his comments on the necessity for leadership in small colleges and the possibilities for someone with some intelligence, a great deal of energy, and a generous supply of imagination at Hartwick.

In Albany I met with the board members and exchanged ideas with them, especially with the Committee on Selection. In fact, I met with the latter committee all evening and until 1 o'clock the next morning. It was about midnight that we mentioned salary and I learned to my astonishment that the president was getting less than $6,000. My earnings as a professor, counting winter and summer sessions and my consultant fees, were more than $9,000. As a result I was offered $9,000 as a salary together with a president's house and necessary expenses.

The Board formally offered me the job, but I refused to accept until I returned to Florida. Then one of the Hartwick professors who was a member of the Selection Committee drove me to Oneonta and I met the retiring president, Dr. Henry J. Arnold, and his gracious wife. I visited the president's home, a somewhat aged but charming house in the middle of Oneonta. The college was on a mountainside overlooking the town. It had only one

3

completed, permanent brick building. Half of another building had been constructed some years before and at that time the chapel wing of this building was under construction. Also, a women's dormitory was under construction. I met faculty members informally and visited with people in town; I looked at the major department store, Bresee's, visited the newspaper office and drove around the town noting the location of the high school and of the State Teachers College. I made the mental note that should I take the job our children would go to the demonstration elementary school there.

At the Albany meeting I had met Mrs. Lauren, a very gracious lady, and her husband, who had been mayor of Oneonta and was the retired president of one of the banks. The Laurens drove me to Binghamton, N. Y., where I visited again briefly with my cousin, Dr. Chrisenberry Ritchie, and his wife and then boarded the plane for Miami.

Fortunately, I have always been able to sleep on a plane, and I slept almost until the plane landed at the Miami airport. I greeted the family at the airport and entertained the children with stories of the little college way up north.

That night Josephine pinned me down for some honest answers. I described everything as accurately as possible, emphasizing the many conflicting factors and winding up with a great big question mark about the whole thing. But to this day she says that she caught a peculiar gleam in my eye and knew that I had been bitten by the presidential bug. Finally she said simply, "If you want to take the job, the children and I will go with you and help."

I conferred with Dr. Pearson, President of the University of Miami, and got not only his good wishes but his blessing in the new undertaking. As Dean of the Faculty of the University, he had hired me six and one half years before. I wired the Trustees at Hartwick that I would accept the job as of July 1.

Although the Hartwick College Selection Committee had contacted a number of sources of candidates and had a very lengthy candidate list, their approach to me was highly unscientific in many respects. They did not even ask whether I knew how to read an annual report nor whether I knew how to build a budget.

4

They seemed to have been impressed by evidence that I had experience in public speaking, that I had been Director of Admissions at Roanoke College, my alma mater, and in many respects general assistant to the president before the war.

They seemed to be almost enamored of the fact that I was chairman of a Human Relations Department and therefore would have the answers to all their community relations problems and money raising problems. It never quite got through to them that my human relations work had been largely the study of intergroup relations (Negro-white, Catholic-Protestant-Jew, social-economic, native-foreign-ethnic).

And one of the most unscientific things they did was to fail to insist that my wife meet with the trustees and some community leaders, particularly the women. They put almost complete faith in the report of Dr. Seybolt that she was an attractive, charming and apparently intelligent wife and mother. They simply assumed that she would be happy in an environment different from any she had experienced and in a completely strange role so long as her husband assumed the presidency.

And on my part, although I appeared to be very thoroughgoing, I accepted the job on faith and, as Josephine has often said, a funny religious feeling of obligation. Instead of just asking about endowment and total amount of the budget, I should have asked about the amount of accounts payable.

I should have had a serious talk with certain faculty members other than those who were on the committee so as to draw them out about the real problems of the institution. I should have asked for the annual reports of the past five years. If I had read them, I certainly would not have taken the job.

But faith is really not a bad ingredient in offering or accepting a job. A certain amount of it is always necessary and there is always the possibility that complete thoroughness in analyzing any job would result in one's refusing it. And, of course, trustees in every case seem to seek a saint and wind up hiring a faulty but eager and possibly courageous human being.

In June I flew to Oneonta to appear at the commencement ceremonies. The ceremonies properly centered about the person and the long service of Dr. Arnold, the retiring president, and the fact that they marked the end of the first quarter of a century of Hartwick as a college. Of course, through its ancestor, Hartwick Seminary, it extended back to 1797. I was called on for brief remarks and spoke only about five minutes. After paying tribute to Dr. Arnold, I wrapped up my own hopes and dreams for the college in the following statement: "We shall build Hartwick College brick by brick, student by student, gift by gift, life by life—together. And this college shall be in our day also a great and good tribute to the past and a shining challenge to the future." After my remarks Dr. Arnold and I stood together and accepted the applause of the commencement audience and shook hands warmly in a show of unity and goodwill. And I am glad to say that this goodwill continued between us throughout the remaining years of his life.

After the ceremonies I caught a plane back to Miami so as to be present for the commencement ceremonies at the University. The children and I attended, accompanied by Grandmother and Grandfather Barnett, and with great pride and pleasure saw Josephine receive her Master's degree from the hands of President Pearson.

The remaining weeks before our trip North were packed with activities, notably my address before the Social Studies section of the convention of the National Education Association in Miami Beach. I spoke on intergroup relations and teacher education and was pleased that the NEA distributed my speech nationally and published excerpts from it in the *NEA Journal*.

Last minute packing, dinner parties by friends and various groups filled our days and nights. Most memorable of these was the reception at the home of Dr. Chelsea Pfarr, an outstanding Negro leader in the community. We had expected 25 or 30 community leaders from the National Conference of Christians and Jews, the Anti-Defamation League of B'nai B'rith, church groups and other groups with which we had worked. We were astonished to find that 300 people had gathered on Dr. Pfarr's spacious lawn to do us honor in an outdoor affair that was a "Miami first" for a mixed Negro and white gathering. Outstanding civic and church leaders of both races were there, including the vice-president of the University of Miami, Dr. H. Franklin Williams.

6

Such pleasant memories as these were very much in our minds as we drove into Oneonta, N. Y., in July with our three small children. Josephine was somewhat discouraged by the rather dismal appearance of the town as we approached it from the south side, but brightened as we drove up delightful, tree-lined Elm Street and stopped before the white, rather charming house. It was locked. But I soon discovered the key in the milkbox. Then we had our first surprise. Our furniture had arrived on time, but it was placed mostly in the wrong rooms so we knew that we had another moving job on our hands. The beds had been set up in the bedrooms, however, and this was the focal point of interest for the tired family, except for our hunger.

I got Norman Roper, business manager at Hartwick, on the telephone, told him of our arrival, hastily refused an invitation to his home and said: "All we want to do is get something to eat and go to bed." It was then about 9 o'clock in the evening. I told him we would especially prefer a drive-in since we looked like "bums." He was nonplussed for a moment and then suggested a place we will never forget, "The Pink Pig," on the outskirts of town. It was a hamburger joint, just what we needed.

We "turned in" for the night feeling much as if we were in a large-sized secondhand furniture store. But we slept the sleep of travel-worn strangers in a strange land.

We spent six years and three months of very satisfying professional and personal life on Oyaron Hill. About three years after we arrived at Hartwick we became convinced that the health of our youngest child, Betsy, who was only two when we arrived, would require our leaving the bitter cold, rugged upstate New York climate. Betsy had a congenital ailment which made her prey to all kinds of respiratory infections. Consequently we let some of our key friends throughout the country know that we would be interested in an appropriate job, not necessarily the presidency, in a mild climate.

Offers came to us from various sources. Some of them were in the Northeast where the climate was, in some cases, really not much better than in Oneonta. One was an approach by members of the selection committee of a somewhat similar but larger college. I said, "Thank you, but I am not interested," without even

7

exchanging letters. The board of trustees of this institution had a bad reputation for interference with administrative functions. This is something every prospective president should investigate. In this case the reputation was so general that I didn't bother to investigate.

Another offer was from the head of a great national agency who promised that I might locate in any part of the country I chose climatewise. But the job entailed almost constant traveling and would disrupt family life completely. This I could not face despite the attractive aspects of the offer.

A friend of mine notified me that the chairman of the board of trustees and the selection committee of a private college in the South would like to interview me. We visited the college within the next few months en route to Florida for a vacation and met with the committee. Almost immediately the question of race relations came out and it was perfectly obvious that the committee would wish me to seek to perpetuate the policy of exclusion of Negro students. This I could not agree to do. Also, a trustee asked if I would include study of communism in Political Science. When I told him I would insist upon it since we ought to know very thoroughly the kind of political forces which were most dangerous to us in the world, he became quite upset.

Despite the favorable climate for Betsy, I knew that we could not possibly live in this kind of collegiate environment. The board subsequently hired as president a professor from a nearby college.

This incident illustrates my very firm belief that a prospective president should discuss frankly points of view with trustees at preliminary meetings so as to make sure to what extent they are in agreement. It is much better to know this ahead of time and to act accordingly. The trustees of this college, which has prospered and grown rapidly in recent years, and I parted friends but in thorough disagreement.

My invitation to the presidency of Pacific University in 1959 was a more careful process but certainly would fall short of an "A" grade as a scientific procedure. In somewhat the same manner as the first contact with Hartwick, a letter came through the mail from a person and a college I had never heard of before. The letter was from James N. Phinney, Assistant to the President at Pacific University, Forest Grove, Oregon. At first I thought the letter was from the University of the Pacific and then remembered that this college was in Stockton, California. The letter asked if I would be interested in the presidency of Pacific University, which was described as one of the oldest colleges in the West and related to the Congregational Church. Incidentally, it is considerably older than the University of the Pacific. Mr. Phinney was serving as secretary of the Selection Committee and was assisting the acting president, Dr. Paul A. Davies, a retired minister and a member of the Board of Trustees. Dr. Charles J. Armstrong had resigned the previous August to accept the presidency of the University of Nevada after having served Pacific for approximately five years as president.

As I learned later, my name had been given to the Selection Committee by an old friend, Dr. E. C. Nance, retired president of the University of Tampa. Dr. Nance was well acquainted in the Northwest and knew of our concern for our daughter Betsy's health and our search for a mild climate. The Oregon coastal region offered of course a mild year-round climate because of the influence of the Japanese ocean currents.

I notified the college that I would be interested in exploring the matter. Shortly thereafter, Ronald M. McCreight, the Chairman of the Finance Committee of the Board of Trustees was in New York City and Josephine and I met him there for a conference. Although we didn't know it at the time, he interviewed several possible candidates on the same trip.

Not long after, I was invited to come to Forest Grove to visit with the Selection Committee and to visit the University itself. I told the University officials that I would come on one condition, that the University would pay my expense and that of my wife and we would bring our children along at our own expense. Since the possibility that we might be interested involved the whole family, I felt it was necessary for the family to be involved in the decision and this is an approach which I recommend to other persons who may be involved in such a decision.

I spent about two days on the campus, visited with the faculty and with key trustees, as well as exploring the community and the lovely Oregon coast. We visited the City of Portland and ob-

9

served its many cultural advantages. The two days on the campus were engaged largely with frank and fruitful give and take with the faculty. I secured printed information that was very essential including copies of the annual report for a number of years back. There were many favorable things about the old University and the delightful community in which it was located as well as the greater Portland area and the coastal region. In fact, personally we were really "sold" on western Oregon as a place to live. But my very thoroughness in respect to the University discouraged me greatly. The almost continuous deficits for many years past, the lamentable condition of buildings, the obvious inadequacy of the faculty and the administrative staff numerically and otherwise were eloquently persuasive in a negative direction.

We went back to Oneonta, after having a delightful trip, quite perplexed and professionally unsold. I checked with my friend, Dr. Theodore A. Distler, Executive Director of the Association of American Colleges, and the net effect of the conference was that I should not take the Pacific job but should wait for greater opportunities in the East. Ted emphasized of course that personal considerations were often more important than professional ones. I, too, was convinced that taking the job was professionally unwise since so many of the problems we had faced and solved at Hartwick were very much in evidence at Pacific. True, there was no extreme financial crisis as had been the case at Hartwick, but rather a chronic, accumulative financially negative situation.

Had the Trustees made no further move, it would probably have ended there. However, soon after we returned from Oneonta a long-distance call from Dr. Davies, the acting president, invited me to return for another visit. Dr. Davies told me that he felt the trustees and faculty had not convinced me on my previous trip, and suggested that I meet with the full Board and alumni leaders, at the expense of the University of course. This I agreed to do.

In the meantime we had continued our own investigation of the Northwest as a place in which to live with the extremely helpful cooperation of our friend Dr. George Davenport Brown, a pediatrician in Berkeley, California. He checked with medical

10

friends of his in the Northwest respecting the climate, the incidence of respiratory diseases, and the various other statistics on health. He knew the University of Oregon Medical Center Hospital very well and the other hospitals in Portland. His report was most positive and he assured us that no healthier place could be found in the United States than the coastal area of Oregon.

The dinner meeting of the board of trustees was well planned. Key trustees and alumni spoke for my benefit on the possibilities of Pacific in relationship to the development of the Northwest. Thomas W. Delzell, chairman of the board of the Portland General Electric Company, spoke of the economic development of the Northwest and was most convincing. James R. Shick, a young lawyer of Forest Grove and a representative of the alumni, assured me of their full cooperation. The distinguished Chairman of the Board of Trustees, Justice George Rossman of the Oregon Supreme Court, brought his great influence to bear. Robert V. Hansberger, new president of Boise Cascade Corporation, was one of the men who impressed me as a real comer in business. His presence on the board was an extremely persuasive factor.

I met with the Executive Committee of the Board after the dinner and they formally offered me the job and urged me to take it. Even so I refused to commit myself. After my return to New York, it took Josephine and me about two more weeks to make up our minds. During that time I called by telephone Dr. Richard H. Sullivan, president of Reed College in Portland, to ask him how he felt about living in Portland and about college life in the Northwest. He was most enthusiastic and verified all the things George Brown had said about the good climate. We checked with former members of the faculty at Pacific who had lived in Forest Grove. They recommended the community and the area as a place to live in highest terms, but corroborated some of my concerns about the college. Of course they agreed that improvements probably had occurred since they were on the faculty.

Finally, we made the decision to go. I had already told Dr. Morris C. Skinner, Chairman of Hartwick's board, what was on our minds. He was most understanding, for he was aware of our personal situation and also knew of our professional happiness at

11

Hartwick which made leaving extremely difficult. I resigned at the May meeting of the Board of Trustees.

The greatest compliment the Hartwick trustees paid me, even more important perhaps than the shining new station wagon they gave us as a going-away present, was an invitation to serve as a consultant to the Selection Committee for my successor. According to many of the books on administration, I should have had nothing to do with the selection of a new president. I chose to accept their invitation not only because of their confidence in me but because Josephine and I had poured so much energy into the little college on Oyaron Hill that I was determined that the next man should be as carefully selected as possible.

A representative committee was set up at my suggestion to conduct the search. I sat down and talked with Wallace R. Klinger, dean of the college and asked him whether he wished to be a candidate, saying that I would suggest him as a member of the committee if he did not wish to be a candidate, but if he were to be a candidate then he should not be on the committee. Wallace talked with his wife about the matter and within a few days informed me that he would stick to the deanship and not be a candidate. Accordingly he became a member of the Selection Committee.

I drew up a list of ten able people and presented them to the committee. From these names and others suggested by various sources we prepared a firm list.

A distinguished dean from a northeastern university was approached by telephone as to whether he would wish to confer with the committee. He turned it down flatly, saying that he was not interested in a college presidency. However, he is now president of a very excellent small college in the East. The second person approached was at the time a vice president of a large southern university. He met with the committee, visited in our home, and was much attracted in many respects, but finally refused.

A third person whom I recommended was the young, brilliant, energetic academic vice president of Thiel College, Dr. Frederick M. Binder. He was 38 years old at the time. I had heard of his excellent work and talked very frankly to the president of Thiel about him. I also checked with other persons whom I felt to be excellent judges of administrative potential. All agreed that he had what it would take to lead Hartwick forward.

We invited Fred and his wife to the campus, giving him full opportunity to examine the college in every possible detail, both through the medium of written material, conferences with the faculty and extended conferences with the Selection Committee and finally with the Board of Trustees.

Although my participation in Fred's selection was unorthodox and I was perfectly aware that I was taking an enormous risk should he fail to meet expectations, I have never had cause to regret it. He did a magnificent job. Under his leadership Hartwick became one of the outstanding small colleges in the Northeast and Fred became recognized as one of the ablest presidents.*

We have now completed our tenth year at Pacific University and our sixteenth year in the presidency. I certainly do not expect to be the primary consideration in another presidential selection. During these ten years at Pacific we have been approached by the selection committees of two other colleges.

One of these is a fine old southern college. Since I was well acquainted with the college and knew members of the selection committee, I accepted the invitation to discuss the matter. In the discussions I criticized rather strongly the lack of effort to get endowment for the institution over the years. Otherwise the institution was in excellent condition. I also raised the serious question of admitting Negroes and got less than satisfactory answers. The trustees did not seem to want to face the situation at the time. At any rate, the conference convinced me that I should remain at Pacific and I think it convinced the committee likewise.

The other approach was from a new college in an extremely attractive area under very challenging conditions. These conditions included a presumption that the college would be highly experimental in nature and would depart from the normal college organization and teaching to a very great extent. The chairman of the board wrote me the letter of inquiry. I took it home to

---

* Dr. Binder resigned as President of Hartwick College on February 10, 1969, to become Associate Commissioner for Higher Education in New York State.

Josephine and we discussed it over lunch and decided the answer would be "no." Subsequently I recommended to the chairman of the board that the college should look for its president among outstanding deans rather than presidents since many presidents would have become "set" in their approach to higher education. Deans would be more inclined to embrace an experimental program. I was interested to learn later that the college had selected an outstanding dean of one of the great liberal arts colleges of the country as its new president.

Would I serve as a consultant to the trustees, if asked, to select my successor at Pacific? I doubt it. It is a risky business. I violated the "taboo" once and had good luck. Perhaps I should not try again.

At any rate, trustees at Pacific are a pretty level-headed lot, and will undoubtedly call for the most expert advice. Actually, before they selected me they had secured recommendations of prospects from college presidents all over the United States and from all sorts of educational agencies and had a total list of fifty which I had seen in the files. My name came into the situation quite late and was suggested, as I have indicated, by a retired president. Anyhow, I am glad they did select me. We have had a great experience here in the Northwest in the service of a historic and at the same time forward looking institution.

I think that the selection of presidents can be greatly improved. It seems to me that representative faculty and student participation is quite necessary. Certainly extensive contact between the prospective parties should take place and the prospective president should have a thoroughgoing, realistic picture of the college he expects to lead. And the same applies in the opposite direction.

It is unfortunate that the protocol of presidential selection historically has meant that the candidates should never make the first move. Somebody must suggest him. The theory, of course, is that a job so important should seek the man. Perhaps so, but there ought to be more adequate ways for the man to be available.

It would seem entirely practical for organizations such as the Association of American Colleges, the organization of presidents in the various religious denominations, the denominational boards of education and the several centers for the study of higher education to have a well annotated listing of promising people who would make good presidents. There ought to be some way so that outstanding deans of administration, academic affairs or development and presidents of smaller colleges could properly submit their names to these organizations so that the powers-that-be in the organizations would know that they are available.

I am quite aware that there are certain placement agencies operated for profit which list presidents, but in most cases the selection committees view them as the last point of reference in the search. It is about time we make the selection of college presidents, if not scientific, at least systematic.

No one should ever accept the college presidency without a compelling sense of commitment to it. Foolish is the person who accepts a presidency because of the automatic prominence it brings, the opportunity for rubbing shoulders with the great and near great, the fact that salaries in the presidency are getting to be respectable. The charm of these advantages will disappear as the new president is faced with the monotonous duties, the impossible problems, and the soul-searching decisions that are also a part of the job. There are many other jobs that offer most of the advantages of the college presidency without the disadvantages and with better pay.

The real attraction to the presidency of a college is the opportunity to be at the center of policymaking in higher education. In many respects I do feel that the presidency should be a "call," as in the ministry, to the individual. Perhaps the job really should seek him. But certainly there are more scientific and systematic ways to bring job and candidate together than have been the general practice in the past.

CHAPTER II

Those Who "Stay Up" the President's Hands[1]

A college president must have a tough mind and a tough body. A timid soul with a fragile frame will not last very long. But a college president needs help—intelligent, imaginative, energetic and loyal help.

Because the job has become so complex, because of the frequent lack of understanding of the job by trustees, sometimes because of the sheer lack of funds, and in some cases because of his own reluctance to delegate responsibility, the college president today is severely overburdened. All too much of the time he is operating under tremendous pressure, harassed to the point of bitterness, unable to do his best at any one thing, and just plain bone-tired.

The late Carter Davidson, shortly after he became president of the Association of American Colleges, was much concerned about this situation as evidenced by this comment: "I shall now try to turn my attention largely to making the lot of the college presidents and deans more attractive, healthy and effective. Too many administrators . . . are killing themselves with overwork in their fifties . . ."[2]

Tragically, Dr. Davidson, after 29 years as president first of Knox College and then of Union College, was not able to ac-

---

[1] The Bible, Exodus 17:12 ". . . and Aaron and Hur stayed up his hands . . ."

[2] The State of the Union 1946-65. Dr. Davidson's last report as President of Union College. Pg. 1.

16

complish his purpose. He died of a heart attack a few short months after becoming head of the Association.

The president's relationship to those who "stay up" his hands varies greatly—from the close, daily teamwork with his private secretary to the occasional conferences with representatives of the firm which prepares the annual audit.

One of the keys to succeeding or even surviving in the presidency is the president's choice of a private secretary. Hers indeed is a difficult role. Although glamour is certainly not a primary essential, she must have appropriate dignity and must present a neat and attractive appearance. She must be able to converse and deal in an equally effective manner with world-renowned visitors and the most recently employed janitor. In the small college the secretary types, takes dictation or transcribes from a dictating machine, and does other clerical duties. Obviously, this work must be of the highest order.

It is important that the president should have a private secretary in whom he has complete confidence and from whom he has complete loyalty. In many respects his secretary is his most confidential professional associate. She must be able to point out errors and save her boss from gross mistakes. She must be able to work under pressure and understand why the office cannot be run on a completely regular, even schedule. She should handle everything in the office the president does not really have to do.

The president's secretary must work closely with his wife so that the quasi-personal role of the president and his wife can be done efficiently and gracefully. In few jobs is there a thinner line between the personal and professional role. This the president's private secretary must understand.

Obviously, a sense of humor is an absolute necessity for a person involved in this type of job. The requirements of the president's secretary are in many respects different from the requirements of other secretaries. Yet, she must be a "good Joe" with all and must not expect unusual benefits and privileges. Even so, it seems to me that the president ought to exempt her from following slavishly the days-off routine of other secretaries and should insist that she have days off at strategic periods to build

17

up her strength for the pressure points of the hectic life of the office.

The day I arrived to take over the president's office at Hartwick College in 1953, I said to the young lady who was my predecessor's secretary: "Tomorrow we must sit down together so that you can instruct me in the routines of this office and get me started on my way. I'll be depending heavily on your experience."

She gave me a very bright smile, but had a puzzled look on her face as she said: "But didn't they tell you I am leaving tomorrow to be married?"

Then followed months of trial and error in trying to get a suitable secretary. I even persuaded my sister-in-law, Mrs. Henry C. Barnett, to come to Oneonta, N. Y., from Cleveland, Ohio, on her vacation to give me some help until a secretary could be found. The several secretaries I tried in my first ten months at Hartwick were very fine people, but young, inexperienced girls who were not really suited to this very exacting job.

Then good fortune smiled. We learned that Mrs. Clara V. Beard, former secretary to the Honorable Joseph P. Leary of Cooperstown, N. Y., had moved to town. She went to work for me on May 2, 1955. And she was a great secretary. Whatever her faults, they are forgotten in the face of excellent work, dealing with confidential matters in confidence, handling the office in my absence with judgment, setting an example for other secretaries without being a "holier-than-thou" bore, and countering my absentmindedness by reminding me to wear my overshoes in the New York snows, to don my raincoat in Oregon, that I must leave a staff meeting to speak to a ladies' club, and that the problem I might be sweating and swearing about really was not as world-shaking as it seemed.

When we came to Pacific University in 1959, my wife urged me to persuade Mrs. Beard to come with us. Josephine knew how much I depend on a good secretary. In May 1965, Mrs. "B" completed her tenth year with the same boss, and Jo and I were hosts at a surprise luncheon for her, complete with a huge cake ablaze with ten candles. All the secretarial personnel of the University were invited. Although the luncheon was intended to express our personal regard and appreciation of Mrs. Beard, it also served to signalize for all those present the important role of the secretarial staff.

In January, 1968, Mrs. Beard retired after nearly thirteen years with me at Hartwick and Pacific. She was succeeded by Mrs. Ruth Langton who is doing an excellent job. I hope she will stay with me until I retire.

Too many colleges try to economize on their secretarial staff. The inefficient results are actually an extravagant waste of funds. It has always been my theory that much more clerical and secretarial help should be given faculty. It seems foolish to pay professors the substantial salaries they demand today only to have them spend much of their time doing stenographic and clerical work any good business school graduate could do better!

Most college presidents whom I know have a special assistant. Undoubtedly this arrangement is sound, enabling the president to conserve his energies and use them for the activities that only he can do.

Frequently the assistant to the president is also a director of development, a public information man, or has other duties. This has been the case in my own experience. It has partly resulted from the fact that in both institutions at the time I became president the administrative staff for public information, development and alumni relations was either non-existent or wholly inadequate. Hence, I enlarged the staff in the most severely needed areas and continued to do directly many things which an assistant could have done for me.

Even after a substantial number of years in the presidency I still find myself taking the direct action when perhaps even more effective work could be done by an assistant. My only comfort is that occasionally I will find a president who is even more detailed in his attention and is not as able as I am in respect to delegation. In some areas of university administration I delegate very readily; in others I still earn poor marks even in my own critical analysis as a delegator.

Obviously the development director is an important member of the president's team. Able leadership in this field is hard to find and it is expensive. One of the "cardinal sins" committed by development directors is their passionate penchant for the mimeograph machine and the mail service. Too often they avoid direct contact in respect to fund-raising, which in most cases is the principal responsibility of the development director.

In college fund-raising there is no substitute for personal contact. And I believe this is true regardless of whether the subject of cultivation is the United States Government, a major or minor private foundation, alumni donors, or a multimillionaire heiress in her eighties with hardening of the arteries! All the letters and literature and meetings and speeches are important, but they are secondary. Someone—the development director, the president, the trustee, the university friend, or the alumni class agent—must directly or indirectly knock at the prospective donor's door and ask for the investment in the college. Of course, unasked-for gifts do come, but they are very exceptional. They should be fervently prayed for and joyfully received when they occur, but they should never be counted on. In my opinion, the biblical injunction, "Ask, and it shall be given you . . . knock and it shall be opened unto you,"[3] is especially applicable to college fund-raising!

In some cases when a university administration changes, the new president brings in an administrative staff of his own choosing. Perhaps this is a good option for him to have. The assumption is that he will bring in people who can work compatibly with him and will respond to his leadership with maximum effectiveness. On the other hand, it is obviously unwise for a president to sweep out all the administrative leadership from former years unless it is inadequate and inferior. There is a need for continuity. There is a need for the president and other administrative leaders to be reminded of the experiences of the past, for it is upon the past that the future must be built.

Obviously the president depends heavily on the good judgment and initiative of the principal administrative dean or provost and the business manager. It is of the utmost importance that these officers know their jobs well and that they relieve the president of concern about details in their areas of responsibility. On the other hand it is equally important that they keep the president informed and secure his counsel and approval on major

---

[3] *The Bible*, Matthew 7:7.

In the early days at Hartwick College and in the absence of money to hire the work done, faculty and students turned to and painted the foyer of Bresee Hall. President Ritchie is shown with a freshman beanie on his head setting an example. On the step-ladder to the left is Miss Edith Lacey, Dean of the School of Nursing, and on the ladder at the far end of the hallway is Gerald Reese, then registrar and director of admissions at Hartwick, currently dean of admissions at Pacific University. Paint had been contributed by local merchants.

Hartwick degree for Senator Jacob Javits. Left to right: Vice-Chairman of the Board of Trustees, Charles L. Ryder; President Ritchie making the conferral; and Dean Wallace R. Klinger, arranging the hood. Attentive on-looker to the extreme right was Dr. Behrend Mehrtens, special assistant to the President for church relations.

Formal acceptance of $250,000 grant from the Dewar Foundation for the building of the second unit of Dewar Hall at Hartwick College. Seated, left to right: Dr. Morris C. Skinner, Chairman of the Board of Trustees and Nathan Pendleton, Treasurer of the Foundation. Standing, left to right: Arthur Seybolt, member of the Board of Trustees; President Ritchie; and Paul Robinson, Secretary of the Board.

President Ritchie is shown with Mrs. Charles W. Leitzell, widow of the second president of Hartwick College, at the cornerstone-laying of Leitzell Hall in 1957 at Hartwick College. Mrs. Leitzell was then in her eighties.

Dr. and Mrs. Ritchie are pictured with Kenneth Buechs, President of the Student Senate, at a farewell luncheon to the President and his wife at Hartwick College in the spring of 1959.

decisions that involve general policy or a serious change in practice that may have far-reaching significance.

In the smaller colleges presidents experience great difficulty in finding the best type of administrative leadership. The public has heard a great deal about the shortage of faculty but little about the shortage of good administrators. For the small college, I believe in gambling on energetic, imaginative young leadership, provided there are enough able, older leaders around to keep the youngsters from shaking the place to pieces!

In both the colleges in which I have served as president, I have hired a number of younger administrators. One obvious reason is that they were available for the price I could pay. A much stronger reason is that they were eager for the job and saw an opportunity to make their mark in a developing career. Gerald Reese came to Hartwick as Registrar and Admissions Director at age twenty three. At the time our new Harvey Scott library at Pacific was dedicated I introduced Louis Flannery as the youngest college librarian in the state. He was thirty-one. The rambunctious "pushiness" of the younger administrators doesn't bother me at all. I like to hear their ideas crackle. They are self-starters. Somebody has to tone them down and keep them within bounds, but nobody has to crank them up to get them started. They are the hope of higher education. In general, taking a chance on them pays for the smaller college.

Although I believe in administrative charts and well-defined responsibilities, I think rigidity should be avoided. The development office should not have to "hatch" all the ideas and prepare all the papers for grants from government agencies or foundations. Relevant academic departments should be pregnant with ideas and eager to establish a case for each application.

Sometimes it is desirable to involve various administrative or academic leaders in tackling a problem so that multiple intellectual resources are tapped. The differing suggestions may make consensus difficult, but often an original idea never dreamt of to begin with will come out of the experience. In the administrative part of a university establishment there should be as much of a ferment of ideas and an appetite for new developments as in any

21

other part of the university or college. Too often this is not the case.

Of course, the development of new ideas presents problems. One of the chief bedevilments of the president can be the young administrator or faculty member who has a brilliant new idea every other morning and insists on a lengthy conference to report it. Unfortunately, in many cases the idea is undeveloped, possibly half-baked, undocumented and often presented in an enthusiastic but thoroughly illogical and confused way.

Frequently the originator of the idea expects the president to take it, develop it, and bring forth a new program to the originator's satisfaction in jig time. In the meantime, he intends to work hard on "hatching" another idea. I've had my share of these sincere and often brilliant eager beavers. The most effective way I have found to harness the often very real talents of the "idea man" is to ask him to bring the idea back in carefully developed form written out with brevity but completeness. Usually the person who is an "idea dilettante" completes the assignment only once or twice and thenceforth discloses his ideas only at the coffee shop to others of similar inclinations. But occasionally a person possessed of a bright new idea is willing to undergo the discipline of developing it, examining the resources to accomplish it, and preparing it in understandable and practical form. Such a person is a real find, and should be recognized and encouraged and possibly appointed to a key administrative post at the first opportunity.

It is my feeling that one of the significant responsibilities of colleges and university presidents is to encourage possible administrative talent among younger faculty and younger men and women who have any penchant for college work. The shortage of administrative talent will increase. Some means of discovering, broadly educating and systematically training in at least a more scientific way than at present the future administrative leadership of our colleges and universities must be found.

If this is not done, Carter Davidson's hope of making the lot of the president at least a tenable one and the effectiveness of the president more adequate to the needs of the times is entirely vain. The administrative staff who "stay up" the president's hands are far more important in higher education than has ever been recognized.

My discussion of those who "stay up" the president's hands began with comment on the highly important role of his private secretary. In practically all cases the president's secretary is a woman, and as such is certainly one of the most important women in his professional life.

If the president is happily married, quite obviously his wife is the most important woman in his personal life. Sometimes it is not generally realized, however, that she is also the most important woman and the most important person in his professional life. The old cliché that a man's wife can make or break him has been worn ragged by overuse, but it is still relevant to a college presidency.

At Hartwick College in 1959 when I served as consultant to the selection committee for my successor, one of the persons I suggested was a distinguished dean of another college. He was a widower. With all proper deference, the trustee committee turned thumbs down. Although the trustees had not been very scientific originally in checking on my wife's potential for the role she was to play at Hartwick, they had come to appreciate keenly the enormous contribution she made and were not about to hire anybody who did not have the strong support of a competent and gracious first lady. Fred Binder, my successor, is blessed with a wonderful wife, and she was a highly successful first lady.

The number of unmarried men selected for college presidencies is quite small. Selection committees simply assume the president's job requires the participation of his wife. Unfortunately, selection committees often assume too much and do not analyze her background to support the assumptions they are making. Consequently, all too often the president's wife comes in for substantial criticism if she does not come up to the assumptions.

I have used the term happily married in reference to the presidency. Certainly a person aspiring to the college presidency who is not happily married should never seriously seek such a job. The presidency is tough enough when there is a happy, satisfying marital relationship and a home environment that reinforces and supports the president in his work. The job cannot be neatly separated from the home as in the case of at least some other occupations.

Even in these days of plush university centers, and competent university culinary staffs, some of the most important campus entertaining is done in the president's home. Obviously, if the president's wife keeps a slovenly house with furnishings and surroundings inappropriate for the entertaining of cultured, sophisticated people, the result is negative. And when there aren't any visitors, an ill-kept household is not conducive to rest and restoration of the tired mind and body of the president.

In my own case I have been fortunate to have a wonderful wife who has made a home which has been a source of both personal and professional strength. My wife really has been my secret weapon. Both of us were children of the depression. We often humorously but quite truthfully say we "consolidated our debts" to get married in June of 1938. We started collecting antiques, not because of the love of antiques, but because our families gave us old furniture. Graduate studies at the College of William and Mary in historic Williamsburg, Virginia, convinced us of the value of these antiques and we have been collecting from second-hand stores and other unlikely places ever since. Consequently our house has practically no two pieces of furniture that match. However, it is loaded with interesting pieces, almost every one of which has a story behind it. Despite the fact that she has always kept a lovely, interesting home, it has always been completely used by the children and by me.

I recall the story of one president whose wife was a particularly fine housekeeper. However, she overdid it a bit. Reading in his study, the president would be interrupted by the telephone and lay aside his book to answer. Returning to his easy chair, he would find his book gone—replaced on the shelf by his wife who had a passion for orderliness! Fortunately, my Josephine is more tolerant.

Every president, in trying to think through his problems, needs someone with whom he can think aloud or nearly so. Sometimes he is fortunate to have a friend or colleague in the profession with whom this is relatively possible. But even so, the person with whom he is likely to "blow off steam" most frequently is his wife. He is fortunate if she is a good listener and if she understands that he really is not going to resign tomorrow and go back to the professorship, the pulpit, or the ranch from which he came! If she has an understanding of the problems of higher education, then she can be his professional as well as his personal confidante. Many an insight for university administration has come into being in such a session between a president and his wife, if she has what it takes!

The college first lady frequently serves as an institutional representative. One of the most difficult tasks for Josephine in our early days at Hartwick was to attend funerals. She was reared a Christian Scientist (now a Congregationalist) and attendance at funerals, especially those whose funeral directors herded the people by the open casket, was extremely difficult. Nonetheless, she was a good soldier and from time to time found herself representing the college at one funeral in Oneonta while I would be serving as honorary pallbearer at a funeral one hundred miles across the state. Many of the friends of the college were elderly and funerals were frequent.

Of course, the president's wife finds herself from time to time facing criticism of the institution and sometimes of her husband. Josephine had such an experience at a women's party shortly before my inauguration at Hartwick. One lady was saying to a group: "I just received an invitation to the inauguration of the new president of Hartwick College and promptly put it in the waste basket. That school is going down the drain anyhow and our town has thrown good money after bad in supporting it. I wouldn't be caught dead at the inauguration." Then she looked at Josephine's horror-stricken face, and after clapping her hand over her mouth and opening it again she said: "Good heavens, you must be the new president's wife."

Josephine said quietly but firmly, "Indeed I am, and we need you and every other person in Oneonta at the inauguration. My husband and I came all the way from Florida on faith to try to build this institution. Certainly you should have enough faith in it and in us to help us."

The critical lady came to the inauguration. She became a friend of the college and our friend. My wife's firmness as a defender of the collegiate faith paid off.

25

Some of us are blessed with first ladies who have special professional values. My wife is a great reader and an excellent student. Through the years she has often done research on forthcoming speeches or articles for me. When important lectures are to be made at meetings she can attend and I cannot, she takes down key points in shorthand and then turns them into neatly typed notes for me when she returns home. Through the years she has never lost her ability at shorthand gained in junior college. From her wide range of reading she supplies me with quotable quotes from significant books and articles of the day.

The president's wife is often the person who "carries the ball" in participating in key community organizations for which the president has insufficient time. In our case Josephine participates in the symphony society, attends the school meetings in our town, and faithfully keeps up with the public issues and makes sure that I do my civic duty and vote.

In Oneonta, N. Y., she was chairman of the Heart Fund, vice president of the Woman's Club, and active in the Garden Club; here in the West she was a founding director of the Tualatin Valley Guidance Center, is a member of the Board of the Mental Health Association and is adviser of the campus chapter of Sigma Alpha Iota.

Especially if a president's wife has given up her own profession in order to become merged as a teammate in the presidency, she ought if possible to have an area of her life in which she is identified separately. Fortunately my wife's activities in the American Association of University Women have supplied some of this need. With this group she served as president of the Oneonta branch and then as president of the Forest Grove branch in Oregon, a member of the Oregon State Board, a member of the National Program Planning Committee, and more recently as chairman of the College Faculty Program in Oregon. In this organization she is recognized as Jo Ritchie, not as the first lady of Pacific University.

But the University has benefitted. And that benefit has not only been in respect to our participation as a college approved by the AAUW and cooperating closely with the local chapter but also in an even more crucial way. Some years ago the head of our

Mathematics Department suddenly resigned late in the spring. The Dean and I made every possible contact, telephoning all over the United States to no avail. But fortune smiled upon us in the person of Dr. Eleanor Dolan, head of the research staff of AAUW in Washington, D.C., who was visiting at the University. I "wept on her shoulder" about the Mathematics situation and she said: "Since your wife works so hard for AAUW, I will make a special effort to see what we can find through AAUW contacts." The result was the employment of Dr. Cecilie Froehlich, formerly professor of mathematics at the City College of New York.

Dr. Froehlich has been a most valued member of our faculty and has brought distinction to the University by virtue of her being a nationally known mathematician. And we owe her to my good wife and her AAUW connection.

Music has been another area of activity somewhat separated from her duties as first lady of the University. As a former music teacher she has attended many professional meetings and institutes on music education. She has been active in the Portland Symphony Society and hosted the organizational meetings of the Forest Grove-Hillsboro Auxiliary.

Several years ago she and a friend, Mrs. Robert Peterson, gave a two-piano recital as a benefit for the Symphony Society. The recital took place at the University Center before a very appreciative audience.

Curiously enough the performance was the possible trigger for an important gift to the University. Since it was a two-piano recital an additional concert grand had to be rented. While conversing with the president of one of the Portland music companies about the rental, Josephine remarked that the University needed another concert grand and that the need would be especially acute when the new concert hall was finished. The next year the same businessman contacted Josephine and informed her that an anonymous donor wished to give the University two Mason and Hamlin concert grand pianos. Just what the initial causal factor was is not known, but obviously the interest in music of the president's wife was involved.

My wife is also my favorite chauffeur. She is an excellent driver and takes the wheel when we are en route to one of my speaking engagements. Often I polish my notes or catch a refreshing nap before reaching the appointed place.

Once during the Hartwick years her chauffeuring was a matter of stark necessity. I enjoy short-order cooking, which I was doing when I burned my left hand very badly. The following week I had four important speaking engagements, one at a Human Relations Institute at the University of Omaha and three in upstate New York. I cancelled the Omaha speech. A substitute expert can always be found. But the others were not so easy. One was the dedication of a new public school near Binghamton involving a key friend of the college. Another was the dedicating address at the opening of a new Jewish Center in Norwich, and the third was a talk to an important businessmen's group.

I made the speeches, with my hand in a huge encasement of bandages and carried in a black sling. Jo drove the car. She said I was never more appealing, illustrating the community interest of colleges and also, incidentally, eloquently testifying to the need of the colleges for help and encouragement.

I am sure that many college presidents would say of their wives something that I recently said about Pacific University's first lady: "In so many ways, she understands education better than I. Without her, I would have given up the college presidency as an impossible job long ago."

But let's not forget the representative of the auditing firm whom we mentioned at the beginning of this chapter. Though he is in a different role from the president's wife, his secretary and some of his other close associates, the auditor is one of those who "stays up" the president's hands. If he doesn't teach the president to read an audit report, someone else has to. When I came to Hartwick, as I have mentioned, I really didn't know how to read such a report, in fact, didn't have enough sophistication to ask to see one before I accepted the job. Contrary to the usual situation the auditor was a woman, Miss Mary M. Mathias. She was a representative of an Albany accounting firm, and with patience and consummate skill taught me about audit reports, translating the figures into intelligent and logical statements. I have been greatly indebted to her through the years. I am no longer frightened by an audit report, though I recognize that it is an

28

important indicator of the health of the institution. Those people who are able to translate these reports for ex-professor presidents are important in the life of the nation's colleges.

The physical environment in which the president and his associates work is important. Obviously, the president should have an adequate office, and it should be located near the development offices, the business manager and the principal deans. One reason for this is the obvious need for close communication back and forth amongst the members of the administrative team.

The president's office should be respectable, comfortable, and properly equipped, but not so luxurious that it is out of keeping with other offices. Some years ago the examination team from the State Department of Education came to Pacific and in its report on teacher education criticized the general physical condition of my office. I was astonished. I had carefully avoided refinishing my office prior to having practically all other offices repainted and refurbished. My office had been completely redone by my predecessor and was in fair condition, but certainly not luxurious.

It is an old office in an old building, and the walls are painted, not paneled. The furniture doesn't all match, but it was and is comfortable and adequate. The chairs and sofa in a conversational corner are real leather! There are abundant bookshelves which please me since I cannot work very well without being surrounded by books. Some of them are actually used!

Whether the one person from the examining committee who came into my office belonged to the misguided group of people who believe that an office should be sumptuously paneled or that it should be completely uncluttered, I don't know. Anyhow, I took this tack in a halfway facetious statement to the local paper from which I quote: "As a former supervisor in a laboratory school of the department of education of the College of William and Mary and as a former member of the faculty of the school of education of the University of Miami, I really don't see any direct connection between a paneled, possibly pretentious president's office and the institution's teacher education program.

"Curiously enough my office has been complimented by many distinguished visitors who are educators, because it is comfortable and somewhat non-institutional looking. As a matter of fact, I have a prayer plant sitting on a small stand beside my desk at the window. It is a beautiful plant and I trust that the committee is not objecting to it. Certainly college presidents stand in need of prayer and the little plant works all the time!!!"

Since the above incident the office has been repainted and improved considerably. New wall-to-wall carpeting has been laid. But I still have retained the beautiful Piranesi prints on the wall. They are old and also rare. And the prayer plant is still hard at work!

The president ought to have adequate equipment and resources in his office. All the reference books, including WHO'S WHO IN AMERICA, that he needs should be provided. On this sort of thing parsimonious economy is out of the question. He should have the best dictating equipment. Some few presidents still dictate to a secretary, but I am a devotee of the dictating machine. All my correspondence is dictated to the machine, which frees my secretary and causes no loss of time. Fortunately, she likes this arrangement and much prefers it to the old-fashioned direct dictation. Occasionally we use the latter method for matters demanding immediate attention. A recent notation in The Gallagher President's Report points out that one dictating machine can do the work of five girls and that a letter dictated to a secretary costs $32.50.

I use the dictating machine for the rough draft of speeches and even for the rough draft of articles written for publication. This method saves a great deal of time. From the dictation machine my secretary has the instructions including notes and references and then constructs the draft of the article or speech for my scrutiny and editing prior to final typing.

In his book ACADEMIC PROCESSION, former President Henry Wriston of Brown University says that every president should have two offices: one into which he can escape from the routines of his life and read, study, write or meditate.[4] I don't have such an office on campus, but use my study at home in this man-

---

[4] Henry M. Wriston: ACADEMIC PROCESSION, Columbia University Press, 1959, New York.

ner. Most of my speeches and articles are prepared here with the help of my extra dictating machine.

In the closet by my desk in the study is a large file. One drawer contains speech notes and speech manuscripts classified. The classified arrangement of notes I started after I became president of Hartwick and discovered what a speech-making routine a college president is expected to follow. Sometimes the same speech will be made at different places. At other times the notes are simply references and a really good speech emerges from two or three sets of notes that represent earlier approaches to the subject.

The familiar stereotype of a president's house is a stately mansion in a remote corner of the campus or just across the street from the campus. The assumption is that it is beautifully furnished, often at the expense of the college in respect to the large reception rooms where social gatherings take place. It generally is expected to represent the best traditions of the region in which the college is situated. Sometimes the president's house is among the earliest buildings on campus.

It is usually assumed that the president's house is staffed by a full-time maid and perhaps a separate person as the cook or sometimes a combination of these two services in one person. Frequently quarters are provided for such staff on the premises. Gardening is likewise taken care of by university maintenance staff or by a special gardener assigned to the grounds of the president's house.

Josephine and I had seen something of this type of arrangement at old Roanoke where we were students and where I was on the staff from 1936 to 1942, at William and Mary where the beautiful old president's house was one of the earliest buildings, at the University of Virginia where the president's house with its stately columns overlooks the campus, and even at the University of Miami where I was a professor. At the last place the president's house is not on the campus, but is nearby and is a very beautiful and spacious residence.

It was something of a shock to us to find that at Hartwick College the president's house was provided, but that was all. No staff, no services. But we were young and did not complain. That

31

is, not immediately. The president's house was off campus and located on one of the older streets in Oneonta. It was charming but badly in need of redecoration, nothing having been done for many years. Also, the kitchen needed modernizing.

A few days after we arrived, the full force of the situation struck us when we had a rainstorm. In the spacious entrance hallway with the winding stairs the water poured through and all the available pots and pans were needed to catch it. My wife lost her poise completely and threatened immediate return to Florida if something wasn't done. A hasty phone call to a trustee who owned a roofing company brought results and a new roof was put on immediately. No wonder the ceilings were stained.

Josephine entered with gusto into the redecorating process and the modernizing of the kitchen. Of course, it necessitated our vacating the house except for sleeping. It was summertime. Every evening I would come down from Oyaron Hill, help Josephine load food and utensils into the car and we would take off for one of the several beautiful picnic parks in Oneonta. I'm sure that the good people of Oneonta to this day do not know that our first real appreciation of their park system came from having our evening meal cooked on one of their grills for at least two weeks of our first sixty days at Hartwick College.

Later, of course, we discovered the ill effects of living in the middle of the city with a postage stamp backyard and no rumpus room since the basement of the house was one of those "bump your head" basements. We had three lively children, and we were in constant holy horror of disturbing the neighbors. Finally, we proposed to the trustees that an allowance be given us so that we might purchase our own house in a more suitable location and that the president's house be sold if an advantageous sale could be made. A sale was made for almost twice what the trustees had originally paid for the house, which, of course, made the Finance Chairman happy.

Unfortunately, however, the trustees in their enthusiasm for the work being done resolved to build a new president's house on the campus. We plainly stated that all we asked for was an allowance, but that we would be happy to have a president's house built on the campus provided it would be adequate to serve presidents in succeeding college generations. Unfortunately, in one of the news stories on future plans for the college, a "president's mansion" was mentioned and this caused much unfavorable comment and undoubtedly we were credited with over-ambitious plans and expensive ideas. We did say that the college should build a thoroughly adequate, handsome, spacious residence on the campus if it were going to build any at all.

The price tag for a house which would fit in with the architecture of the campus and meet the needs of extensive entertaining of students and visitors was placed at about $60,000. This was too much for the trustees, and they agreed to an allowance instead. Consequently we bought a very attractive home on the edge of town, adjacent to the golf course with plenty of space for our children and with perfectly adequate accommodations for our family. The house was not adequate for presidential entertaining and never would be, but personally we could not afford the kind of house that would satisfy this requirement. Hence, a good bit of our entertaining was done at the country club and at the college after the new Commons was built. Even so, we had various receptions and parties at our house, handling guests on an alphabetical basis in order to enable a house of relatively modest size to accommodate them.

When Pacific University was courting us, we flatly said we would not live in the old president's house which is situated in the midst of the campus and is a most unattractive house architecturally. The trustee committee did not hesitate in agreeing and provided a perfectly adequate allowance to make it possible to purchase a home of our own in the community. The catch was that the town did not have houses of adequate size within the price range we could pay. One home of adequate size was available at $53,000, but this was beyond our means. Finally, on my third trip to Pacific before our move there, I learned by accident that Mrs. Joseph R. McCready might be willing to sell her house. The late Joseph R. McCready had been a trustee at the University.

The house is of colonial architecture, surrounded by a beautiful lawn, and has five bedrooms. This was adequate for our needs and would make possible entertaining of overnight university guests from time to time. The living-dining areas are not sufficiently large for some types of entertaining, but adequate for most.

Josephine actually agreed to the purchase sight unseen so far as the interior of the house was concerned. She had seen the exterior on our earlier trip together and had admired the property. Of course, I had my fingers crossed when she first crossed the threshold. Then she said: "It'll be fine; our furniture will be at home."

But moving in wasn't as simple as moving into an empty and carefully prepared university president's residence. We had to arrive by the first of September to put the children in school. The house was not available until about the middle of September. Consequently, we "camped out" in the women's dormitory until the house was available, storing the furniture in Mrs. McCready's garage and basement of the house. Thus we had really two movings to accomplish—moving across the country and then moving the furniture from the garage and from the basement upstairs and all over the house.

During our ten years of living here, we have enjoyed the property and have blessed Mrs. McCready for her good taste. Only one room had to be redecorated due to the fact that the furnishings and draperies clashed. From time to time I have cursed the extensive flowerbeds and plantings in the yard, for they have demanded a lot of care. Although I am an avid gardener, which helps to qualify me as an adopted Oregonian, my schedule is such that I cannot be consistent in my work in the garden. So I hire special help on the weekends. Often I say if I just had half as many flowerbeds and plantings I would be much happier. But the fact that we are seven blocks away from the campus, that there are seven great oaks in the backyard and that we have a high degree of privacy and quietude, makes up for any other drawbacks.

Daughter Betsy stabled her horse about a block from our house. This would have been impossible on campus or in other parts of town. Our property is just on the edge of the town, one block from the county line. It is really country living with town conveniences. We can entertain students and others for we are within easy walking distance from the campus, but people do not casually drop in unless they really want to see us. This, too, is a blessing.

What I have said, at least in part, has argued the case for an allowance to the president and for a house away from campus. But I have no special brief for this as university policy. An adequate house near the campus or on the edge of the campus from the standpoint of the university is probably better. And the major reason is that the president, unless he is a man of means, really cannot afford the kind of home that ought to be the official residence. And an official residence tends to prestructure and set expectations for the role the president and his wife play. Visitors to the campus may be entertained royally at the university center, but there is nothing quite as effective as a cup of coffee or tea or a glass of Oregon cranberry juice in the home of the president. This is the personal touch that more than once has made considerable difference in the cultivation of friends of a college.

But an official residence has caused many a controversy. Some years ago a new president came to Oregon State University. The retiring president stayed on with the state system of higher education and was given the privilege of continued occupancy of the old president's house. Consequently a new president's house was built costing substantial money. A veritable stream of abuse was poured upon the University and the innocent and un-offending new president and his wife. Newspaper stories describing the criticism indicated all too well the total lack of public appreciation of the difficult role the president of a great state university plays. Not only the subtle nuances of this public-private role went unappreciated, but even the more obvious functions of entertainment and hospitality were overlooked in the harsh allegations of extravagance made against Oregon State. Fortunately, the powers that be in the state system held firm and an attractive and adequate president's house was provided.

I am sure that the distinguished and warmhearted service that Dr. and Mrs. James Jensen have rendered to the University has in part been made possible by the excellent president's house which they have enjoyed and generously shared with the University faculty, students and friends.

I certainly do not expect again to be deciding on the matter of a president's house and the things that should go with it. But if I were a younger man, invited to a presidency, I think I would refuse it unless an entirely adequate house were provided or a very generous allowance in lieu of it, together with full-time maid service and complete grounds maintenance. The presidency makes peculiar demands on the president, his wife and family. It is neither wholly public nor wholly private; it is mixed. The requirements for doing a good job are very special. The importance of the provision and maintenance of an entirely adequate home environment and services does not really become clear until one has occupied the office for a number of years.

It is not the fault of trustees. They cannot be expected to understand these needs. It is really the responsibility of us who are experienced presidents to state these needs clearly and frankly and so to advise the younger fry who will be the new presidents on campuses all over America in the future.

It has been said that a university is the lengthening shadow of one man, the president. I disagree. It is the lengthening shadow of a whole procession of people. Especially those people, to use again the sturdy biblical words, who "Stay up" his hands. And I would add, those people who provide him the environment and equipment with which to do his job.

CHAPTER III

Ascending the Holy Heights

College presidents, by the nature of their offices, lead exemplary lives. Sometimes in his highest moments of service, a college president may seem to be a Moses on a mountaintop receiving the Law directly from God. At other times he may be considered a popular, pseudo-virtuous, conforming fellow nimbly balancing himself on a pedestal and enjoying at least for the moment the praise and approval of his fellows. In a different period or situation he may be held aloft on the spear points of his enemies when all he can hear may be the scathing denunciations of those who now believe him to be a has-been scholar, an administrative charlatan who tries to please everybody and tells the truth to none, and a persistent pickpocket who would sell his soul for the cornerstone of a new building. Perhaps such dramatic description does not apply to every college president, but it is certainly true that he can seldom be simply a private person. He may head a private college, but his role is largely non-private.

So far as ceremonial occasions are concerned, the inauguration of a new president is one of the most impressive. On this occasion he formally "ascends the holy heights" and assumes the solemn responsibilities of his office before one of the largest audiences of his students, academic peers and supporters he will ever face.

There are those who are critical of inaugurations and feel that they should be abolished. I think they are good but could be improved. I recall that the late Malcolm Ross, editor and father of the University of Miami Press, urged that I make sure to capitalize on the inauguration in my first presidency at Hartwick. Said he: "At no other time in your administration will you be able to collect for your college so much favorable, almost automatic, public notice for so little an outlay of money as you can with a well-done inauguration." It was sound advice.

Usually inaugurations are held some time during the first year of the president's service at a college. This enables him to get a staff and to get well established and acquainted before the inauguration takes place. It also enables him to have some role in the planning. It should be remembered that the inauguration is not for him; it is for the institution. It is not to cultivate his ego but to improve the image of the college and possibly to make some contribution to higher education generally.

Other colleges throughout the country or at least regionally are invited to send representatives to the inauguration. These representatives may be the president or the chairman of the board of trustees of the institution or they may be alumni living in the community where the new college president is to be inaugurated. Usually a substantial percentage of the representatives are alumni of the institution to be represented rather than administrative officers. This is a good thing in many respects. It means that a large cross section of population of the area in which the institution operates will be represented at the inauguration of the new president and will be brought into closer contact with the institution.

Usually there is a principal speaker for an inauguration. Sometimes a couple of days are set aside for panel discussions, seminars and the like relating to some major topic on higher education. In general for the smaller colleges, inaugurations usually are concentrated in one day's major program. In addition to the principal speaker there is the formal investiture of the president and a speech by him. Oftentimes this address gives some hint of his policies for the institution or at least the direction in which he expects to lead it. Of course, the delegates participate in a colorful academic procession. Frequently there is a luncheon for all the delegates and sometimes there is a religious service. Familiar, also, are the inaugural reception and the inaugural ball.

Newspapers and other mass media usually are generously cooperative in covering inaugurations. A number of feature articles as well as regular news coverage on noted personages will appear in the local press. Radio and television coverage is good. The history of the institution or its special contributions to the welfare of the community, state or nation can be stressed.

Preparation for an inauguration can be an onerous task, but on the other hand it can be an opportunity to involve a large number of persons who might otherwise not be active. It provides an opportunity for the president to work closely with an inaugural committee; sometimes it is the first major common task he performs with a cross section of administration and faculty. At other times this dimension of cooperation is extended to the community.

In my initial analysis of the problems of Hartwick College, I noted a substantial lack of confidence in the institution on the part of Oneonta citizens. Attendance at college functions was poor. Contributions, although there had been a number of generous individual donors, generally were few and far between. In discussing the inauguration with Dr. H. Claude Hardy, director of public relations, I raised the question of choosing a chairman for the inauguration from among the prominent citizens of the community rather than the usual procedure of naming someone on the faculty as a chairman. Dr. Hardy's reaction was positive and he agreed that such a procedure might help to identify the community leadership with the college in a favorable manner.

After discussing a number of possible chairmen, Dr. Hardy introduced me to Mr. Charles House, the area supervisor of the D & H Railroad. Mr. House accepted and gathered around him a committee of citizens to work with faculty members in setting up the plans for the inauguration. A great deal of community involvement followed and we had reason to be very well satisfied with the somewhat novel arrangement.

The actual inaugural ceremonies took place on the campus, but the luncheon took place at the city armory. Automobile dealers from the town furnished fleets of cars to provide transportation back and forth. Participation of citizens created lively discussion about the inauguration with resulting excellent attendance both for the ceremonies and for the luncheon. Hartwick College needed a public relations shot in the arm and the inauguration certainly provided it.

At the actual ceremonies we carefully involved not only the

faculty and the community, but also the supporting church. The speaker, however, we chose on a more ecumenical basis. He was Dr. Everett R. Clinchy, president of the National Conference of Christians and Jews, and an ordained Presbyterian minister. Dr. Clinchy is one of the most noted men in America, now retired from his presidency of NCCJ. His address and his presence made a positive contribution in the direction of support of Hartwick from many different groups. Although his serving as inaugural speaker brought some criticism, as described in Chapter IV, the general response to his participation was most positive. He had been a friend of mine for a number of years and I not only personally desired his participation but felt that his contribution would be a substantial one intellectually and otherwise.

At Pacific University my inauguration came in the spring following my becoming president in the fall. Old Pacific needed to give the public assurance that it had new and vigorous administrative leadership since it had been without a president for a year during which time it had operated under an administrative committee and an acting president. Invitations were sent to colleges and learned societies throughout the country and approximately 200 official delegates attended the inauguration as well as a vast crowd of well-wishers. Many of the delegates representing other colleges were from the city of Portland. Some of them for the first time thus became interested in and slightly connected with Pacific University.

The guest speaker for the inauguration was the Honorable William F. Quinn, Governor of Hawaii. He made a statesmanlike address recognizing the merits of higher institutions such as Pacific University and emphasizing the importance of their support. In addition to his address at the inaugural ceremonies, we had Dr. Stuart Anderson, president of the Pacific School of Religion, as guest speaker for a special religious service.

Bill Quinn is an exceedingly interesting and attractive person and well known to the people in the Northwest in view of his being the last appointed Governor of the Territory of Hawaii and the first elected Governor of the State of Hawaii. The press covered his visit fully and favorably. And incidentally, the University received vast amounts of public notice which would not have ordinarily been the case.

As at Hartwick, we engaged the cooperation of the business leadership of our community. This time we did not have a local businessman as the chairman of the inaugural committee, but we asked the Chamber of Commerce to organize a Governors' Luncheon the Monday following the inauguration on Sunday. The reason it was called the Governors' Luncheon is that Governor Mark Hatfield of Oregon was present as well as Governor Quinn. He also was present for the inauguration on Sunday and introduced Governor Quinn.

The Chamber did a great job on this project and several hundred businessmen from all over Oregon attended the Governors' Luncheon, paying for their own transportation to come to Pacific University, to hear Bill Quinn, and incidentally to get involved with our institution. The Royal Rosarians of Portland were present and surprised both Bill Quinn and me by knighting each of us as one of their remarkable Order, devoted to publicizing Portland as the City of Roses. Mayor Terry Shrunk was present and presented me with a live rose bush which I planted the next day in my yard and from which I have been cutting beautiful roses ever since. Another interesting touch for the inauguration was the sheriff's mounted posse from Washington County. These gentlemen, riding beautiful horses, helped to direct traffic and also give a bit of western color to the affair.

Even the weather provided drama in that we had a most unseasonable snowstorm two or three days before the inauguration. A substantial amount of the snow still remained on the ground during the great day. Ordinarily in Oregon we do not have snow on the ground on March 6.

One of the interesting and amusing aftermaths of the inauguration was a report circulated among the students that the University had spent $10,000 on the affair. Of course, this was completely false. We did things nicely and in proper style, but the total bill was certainly not over $2,000 and the public attention that the University got through the country was, of course, worth many, many thousands of dollars. The students assumed that it cost a great deal to get Governor Quinn, but actually he accepted no honorarium at all, submitting only a modest travel expense account.

My inaugural address was probably more remarkable for its brevity than anything else. I spoke approximately twelve and one half minutes. In some ways, however, the address did give insight into the kind of leadership I proposed to give Pacific University as indicated by the following quotes:

"As long as I am president of Pacific University I shall encourage intellectual development of a higher order, and I know that my colleagues on the faculty will not have to be persuaded in that direction.

"But sheer intellectual development is not enough! To be constructive in society brilliant intellects must be undergirded by positive moral and spiritual values.

"I am persuaded that excellence is pertinent to the social as well as to the academic life of the campus.

"By excellence in religious commitment I do not mean a narrowly defined faith and compulsory chapel attendance! I mean commitment to the idea that religion as a phenomenon in human life is a respectable subject for study and should be an offering in a college or university curriculum. I mean commitment to giving students opportunity to consider the ideas of great religious leaders of many faiths. I mean commitment to the idea that the college which calls itself Christian should practice some of the implications thereof, whether they refer to the sanctity of individual personality, to sending books to Korea, or to opening the college doors to persons of all races, religions and nationalities. Too often religious commitment in a college never gets more intellectual than propaganda for a particular faith, never really relates itself to social needs, and never quite disassociates its vision from the total annual monetary apportionment of the supporting church.

"After more than a quarter of a century in education, I am increasingly convinced that a high degree of excellence in the intellectual, social, and spiritual dimensions of education is most likely when the student has a strong sense of community—when he feels he belongs, is recognized, and counts for something significant in the college group. The relatively small college has peculiar fitness to give him such a sense of community.

"In order to be a major resource, however, small colleges have got to set their house in order. They are generally woefully inefficient and wasteful in the use of time, space and manpower, and should revise their practice.

"Smaller colleges should quit destructive and needless duplication of programs. Cooperative small college foundations for fund raising have become highly successful. The same principle should be put to work in other areas of college life."

From the time he is inaugurated and from the very first day he takes office a college president is engaged in public interpretation. It is one of his major functions. A substantial portion of the president's time is spent or should be spent in preparing for this role, for both he and his institution will be judged favorably or unfavorably by his performance.

Public speaking of one kind or another is a major means of public interpretation. If he is a good speaker, invitations will crowd in upon the president, and if he isn't careful he will be constantly on the platform. Indiscriminate speechmaking will soon overexpose him, exhaust his powers, and eat up his store of significant information or ideas. Sooner or later he must learn to make wise choices among opportunities and to make the most of those he does accept. In accepting speaking engagements the president should refuse to speak on topics on which he has nothing significant to say. Since he cannot accept all of his invitations, he should accept those engagements which will benefit the college most.

Sometimes speechmaking can play an important role in bringing favorable notice to a college that has not had too much of it previously. After I became president of Hartwick College, one of the trustees urged me to try to get before key education groups and business groups, since the enrollment of the college was at such a low ebb. Fortunately, I was already on the list of a national lecture bureau in Washington, D.C. Shortly after I came to Hartwick I was placed on the speakers' list of Program Associates, Utica, New York. My arrangement with this lecture bureau permitted selective acceptance of engagements.

I accepted all possible engagements before educational bodies, such as meetings of the New York State Education Association, school board conventions, and area teachers' institutes. I also accepted numerous commencement engagements, one spring doing nine commencement addresses, including two colleges. In addition I spoke before church groups and businessmen's organizations including two major meetings of leading businessmen at the Waldorf-Astoria in New York City.

The trustees could not have been more delighted, for the lecture bureau not only paid me a fee sufficient to defray my travel expenses but also gave me something in addition. The favorable reaction was obvious. The admissions director of the college took care to follow up in the areas where I had addressed public school groups so as to capitalize on the interest developed. These groups keenly appreciated hearing a private college president express concern and interest in matters of public education.

When speaking frequently in public and from a variety of platforms, a college president learns the importance of cooperation with the press, radio and television. Reporters will appear in unexpected places to cover an address and at other times when most expected will not appear. When speaking from notes I developed the practice of carrying a sheet or two of quotations along so that when the press representatives contact me before or even after a meeting I have something available. In ninety percent of the cases the press representatives are delighted to use the prepared quotations, thus avoiding substantial possibility of error.

Oftentimes a minimum of effort will produce excellent press coverage. When scheduled to give the annual dinner address of the National Conference of Christians and Jews in Portland, Oregon, in 1965, I had my secretary prepare additional copies of my address which the executive director of the organization distributed to the press, radio and television. The result was full and accurate coverage in all media. The following year, in my opinion, the speaker made a much better address than mine, but very little appeared in the newspapers because advance copies of the address were not available to the reporters.

Even a relatively local group may sometimes be the setting for an address that will attract wide attention. Sometime after the student disturbances on the Berkeley campus of the University of California I was invited to address the Beaverton Rotary Club. I chose as my topic, "The Small College: A Partial Answer to Berkeley!" The Public Information Office sent advance copies of this address to the newspapers and to radio and television stations. I was surprised and gratified that a major television station sent a reporter-cameraman team to Beaverton to cover my address. Other stations handled the matter differently, but there was excellent coverage in all mass media despite the fact that my address was really a routine Rotary program.

The college president who looks down his nose and has no time to bother with the hardworking representatives of newspapers, radio and television stations is certainly not going to get good coverage and will seriously jeopardize his opportunity to interpret higher education adequately and effectively to the public. Responsible reporters, feature writers and commentators appreciate very keenly the president who will see that his office or the proper office on a college campus takes the trouble to dig up pertinent facts for accurate and informative coverage.

Strangely enough, some of the most shortsighted attitudes on the part of presidents occur in connection with the television. Several years ago I was involved on a committee to plan a series of television programs to publicize the private colleges of Oregon. Miss Gloria Chandler, public service director of the King Broadcasting stations, was conferring with us. We were discussing the problem of portraying a seminar class typifying the work of the small colleges on the television. Another president and I found ourselves in a very hot argument because he insisted that the television programs should pick up the seminar at the beginning of its hour-long discussion and continue all the way through to the end. He could not possibly accept the notion that for television we would have to pick up the discussion at the highest point of interest and perhaps show only a portion of the discussion. Assuring him that the boring warmup would likely mean that thousands of people would snap off their televisions or switch to another channel seemed to have little effect.

One of the great failures in public interpretation on the part of college presidents has been a lack of cooperation with public service directors of television stations who have been more than

45

willing to develop programming on higher education, provided it is interesting and stimulating for the listening and viewing audience. Radio and television are powerful means for sound interpretation of higher education, but thus far they have not been adequately understood nor used by college presidents.

One of the hazards of the presidency is becoming so involved in the busy work of administration that creative thinking is crowded out. The story is told of the college president who had fallen victim to this trap and one day came into his office to open his mail and found there was none that particular day. He exclaimed in consternation: "My God, I'll have to think." Too many presidents become completely alienated from the discipline in which they once were excellent professors. In some cases at least they have almost ceased to read and have failed to keep their intellectual batteries charged. As a consequence their creative powers are dead.

Whenever possible, it is of great value for presidents to retain some connection with their discipline. In rare instances presidents are able to teach a class, perhaps a seminar, once a week or more. Of course, in most cases on most campuses this is impossible because of the increasing complexity of the job.

In my own case a useful practice has been that of accepting from time to time lecture assignments in the field of social science, especially in intergroup relations. These lecture assignments have required me to keep up at least in part with the literature in the field. Some of these lectures have been published by different organizations.

Presidents complain about not having opportunity to read, and I can certainly appreciate the complaint. Though there is always a book on my bedroom table, I am often too "dog tired" to read after getting home late at night. However, there also is likely to be a book or two in my attaché case if I am on a trip. I find that a great deal of reading can be accomplished on flights across the country, at odd times in airports, and in many other circumstances where the time ordinarily would be whiled away in idle conversation with some other passenger. At every opportunity I do read at night or whenever possible at home. A president really should budget time for reading and studying and thinking. If he can, he should simply disappear into his home study or to some other place and refresh his mind with other people's ideas.

Another popular assumption is that presidents never find time to write for publication. Odd moments on plane trips and time deliberately budgeted from the regular daily routine can produce thoughtful articles, provided the president has done the reading, the observing and the thinking that are required. Of course, this applies to the writing of speeches, some of which may become articles in edited or amended form in professional journals. If it is fair to say that a professor is obligated to put his ideas before his peers instead of restricting himself to the captive audience of his students, then it is fair to say the same thing of a president.

Many presidents, it seems to me, unnecessarily wear themselves out going to every professional meeting to which they are invited. Whenever appropriate, I believe it is good practice to send administrative deans or other university officials. They almost invariably respond with enthusiasm and get a sense of deepened responsibility by representing the institution. It does appear, however, that some presidents really enjoy being hurried, harassed, convention-goers!

College presidents are automatically considered community leaders, and they have an inescapable responsibility to make a reasonable contribution of time and energy. But the president should exercise judgment in serving on boards and committees where his background and ability can do some good. He should avoid such an overload of community leadership that this activity interferes seriously with his college duties. It is, of course, recognized by administrators that service in key community groups is a major way of interpreting education to the community as well as a major way of identifying with other community leaders so as to be in a position to involve them in the life of the college. Many an able trustee and sometimes a generous donor is first contacted by the president as he works on a community project of common concern.

General participation in the community by the president and his family is not only desirable but expected. But this participation is not quite as carefree as for the average citizen. Often the president's church affiliation and his participation are to some extent determined by denominational sponsorship of the college. There are those who would favor very vigorous activity and office holding by the president in his church. I tend to feel that faithful attendance and loyal service on committees may be in order, but I have concluded that a key leadership role by the president in the local church is undesirable. Such a role frequently involves him in relatively unimportant but sometimes disastrous tests of strength and choosing of sides. Further, if the college is relatively liberal in its attitudes and not dominated by the church to which it is related, the president in many respects belongs to all the churches and should make manifest his interest in the people of various other denominations and his appreciation of the way in which they express themselves religiously.

It is a common assumption that the destiny of colleges financially and otherwise is often decided at the 6th or the 9th or the 18th golf green. If the president enjoys golf he should by all means play. It is a healthful recreation, and he may make valuable contacts for his college and may profit greatly by the pleasant association with other golfers. But for the president to spend whole afternoons chasing a little white ball with a stick all over the countryside in order to make the magic contact with a millionaire is a bit far-fetched. I believe that more sizeable donations are secured over the lunch table, in the donor's office, at his home, or standing on the campus and looking the needs of the college in the face than is the case on a golf course.

To drink or not to drink—at a small party at home or at the bar downtown with the boys—often is a perplexing question to a new president, especially if he is the head of a church-related college with a fairly conservative outlook. Of course, social drinking by college presidents today is so customary that no one engages in the harsh criticisms of years gone by. Yet it can pose some problems.

In our own case, my wife and I discussed the matter quite seriously in my first presidency. The college was church-related. It had a no-drinking rule for students. Some of its supporters, constituents, trustees, alumni and friends drank, others did not.

In view of the no-drinking rule at the college, we felt the

least complicated approach would be rigorously to avoid serving any kind of liquor, even wine, at any function in our own home. We held to this rule and still do. It has had the effect of providing an example of abstinence that has been a strength in respect to drinking among students and faculty. In a way it is unfortunate that this practice has tended to label us as complete teetotalers and we have been given credit for being opposed to any drinking whatever. Yet we have never said that we are teetotalers, nor have we ever suggested that having a glass of wine or a cocktail constitutes a one-way ticket to hell-fire. It has just seemed a great deal simpler to handle the matter this way and I suppose we will probably continue to do so.

One of my friendly administrative critics at Hartwick suggested strongly to me that I missed a great many wonderful contacts and possible donations to the college by not "lifting the elbow" in the local bars and at the weekend parties at the country club. He may have been right in some cases. However, it was my feeling that most of the individuals who gave very substantial sums to Hartwick College while I was president approved the example we set and perhaps were more inclined to give money because of it than in spite of it.

College presidents are invited to perform on almost any imaginable program and to engage in a weird variety of activities. At Oneonta I recall being invited to judge a beauty contest. Courteously but firmly I refused. In my first year at Pacific University I was invited to judge a beard contest. Again I courteously but firmly refused. It isn't that I dislike beautiful gals who participate in beauty contests and vigorous men who compete with beards. It is simply that I feel that college presidents cannot do everything and that they should draw a line excluding a great many miscellaneous activities that are not calculated to be of great help to the institution. If once the president judges a beauty contest or a beard-growing contest, the gate is wide open for every conceivable function and when he finally does start refusing he will bruise the feelings of half the community.

The question of political participation and leadership is just as pertinent to presidents as to professors. Of course, the president should exercise his civic duty by voting for candidates of his choice and by membership in the party in whose principles he believes. And he should defend the right of his professors likewise to participate. Further, he certainly has the right to stand for political office unless his trustees have obligated him otherwise and unless the duties interfere with his performing university functions. The same, in my view, applies to faculty.

At Pacific University several faculty members during my presidency so far have held responsible local political offices, one being a Mayor of the city of Forest Grove for a dozen years or more. One professor currently sits on the county commission. Various criticisms have been voiced to the effect that college professors ought to stay out of politics. I have stoutly defended the right of professors to participate and to run for political office provided that holding such office does not interfere with university duties and that they run as individuals and not as representatives of the institution.

Having said the above in favor of participation, I should add that I believe a college president is in a stronger position to support or oppose, praise or criticize, either party or both if he is not an active elective office holder and if he has not taken a prominent role in partisan politics. It seems to me that taking a highly partisan role involves loyalty to a party and limits the opportunity for healthy and frank criticism by the president of the political leader or political party. And on occasion political parties do have a very strong influence upon the success or failure of university programs whether they be public or private. The president as the representative of the institution as a whole should be in a position for maximum influence in the community for the programs considered positive for higher education.

Some years ago I was asked to be local co-chairman of the campaign of a very able man for United States senator. Regretfully I refused on the grounds I just stated. I admire this person very much indeed and would gladly have worked hard for him if I did not feel so strongly the soundness of this position. However, I realize that many other college presidents take different views and I recognize their right to hold those views. Dr. Arthur Flemming, former president of the University of Oregon and a former cabinet member under President Eisenhower, was an active

Republican leader in Oregon and in the nation since returning to university administration. Many years ago Columbia's Nicholas Murray Butler was proposed as a possible candidate for Vice President of the United States. And, of course, Dwight Eisenhower himself was president of Columbia University on leave when he became a candidate for the Republican nomination.

The college president who has a heart as well as a head and a tough hide finds himself often in the role of personal counselor. Often he and his wife must be comforters to bereaved families. The role of honorary pallbearer is a familiar one. Like the minister and his wife, the president and his wife must give what comfort they can when tragedy strikes in trustee, faculty, or student homes and often in the homes of other friends of the college. With us there was the question of what to say but we soon found that words are not terribly important. The proffered help, the presence, the attitude, are deeply appreciated by those bereaved.

Several years ago two fine young students at Pacific University were in a terrible automobile accident. One was killed, the other injured. Josephine and I omitted appearance at an important university function in order to go to the hospital to see the surviving young man and to comfort him not only because of his own injuries but because of his concern about being spared when his good friend was gone. And then the next day, the parents of the dead boy came to our home to express thanks to the university for all that had been done and especially to thank us for our attention to the surviving boy and to report that they likewise had sought to bring cheer and comfort to him.

At Hartwick there was a distinguished professor with whom I was not particularly close. And this was also true with his wife, a brilliant woman. Then suddenly death took their only son and they were emotionally crushed. Josephine and I visited their home, offered sympathy, very awkwardly we thought and very inadequately, but out of it came a close relationship between the father and me in which he sought counsel and help respecting his distraught wife. We learned to know both as wonderful, warm, devoted people as well as intellectuals.

The college president's job these days is so complex that no longer can he be a friend to all students nor call too many of them by name, but he is still turned to in a surprising number of cases by people young and old who somehow suppose that he is a man of sympathy, insight and faith.

If a prospective college president is not adept at letterwriting and does not enjoy this mode of communication, he had better get some other kind of job. The correspondence of the president is enormous. He receives mail by the ton. Sometime ago I received a request from a man in West Virginia for a photograph and autograph with a brief biography. The writer was making a kind of "rogue's gallery" of college presidents. School youngsters often from a great distance write for some comment about life in general or particular. Of course, there is much routine mail that the secretary or an assistant can handle.

But the ability to carry on a lively, interesting correspondence with hundreds of people is indispensable to the presidency. The letter of condolence or the letter to the new friend who shares with the president an interest in gardening may be a part of his morning's work as well as the application to a foundation, the formal contractual letter to a new professor, or the diplomatic note to the griping parent or perennial critic. Unless they are letters to old friends or unless they are in answer to specific questions, letters generally should not exceed one page!

Letterwriting to me has never been a serious chore, though I do complain about the more routine ones. Yet, I do not delegate as much letterwriting as I might. To me dictating letters is simply conversation on paper. This attitude is enormously helpful in enabling me to get started promptly and to avoid undue worry about literary polish. Soon after beginning the presidency I realized that it was much better to get the imperfect letter off on Tuesday than to get the perfect letter off on Friday, too late to have maximum effect. One of the first lessons a president must learn is that he simply cannot wait upon perfection. The nature of the job probably makes the college president one of the most imperfect of human beings and his letterwriting is one place this will certainly show.

Really, I don't think I will ever be too sophisticated to get a thrill out of dictating letters in one morning to alumni in the Orient, in Africa and in Europe. And I sometimes get an even

At the Graduation ceremonies marking the completion of the 120th year of Pacific University, Dr. Ritchie is shown presenting the President's Trophy to William H. Hedgebeth, in recognition of his achievement of the highest grade point average in the senior class.

At Hartwick College Josephine Ritchie is shown playing hostess to Louis "Satchmo" Armstrong who gave a student-senate sponsored concert in 1957-58. Just behind Mr. Armstrong are Mr. and Mrs. Ralph Larson.

Two friends in earnest conversation at a Pacific University dinner: Oregon Senator Mark O. Hatfield and President Ritchie. Senator Hatfield made the principal address at the mid-year commencement and Founders Day ceremony December 18, 1966, and received a Doctor of Laws degree.

Groundbreaking team for the new College of Optometry building, Pacific University, October 30, 1965; (left to right) Trustee Dr. Roy Clunes, Optometry Dean Dr. William R. Baldwin, Trustee Louis P. Busch, Trustee Dr. Clary Carkner, President Ritchie, Trustee Chairman Ronald M. McCreight.

Commencement speaker at Pacific University in May of 1966 was Hobart Taylor, Director of the Export-Import Bank, Washington, D.C. He is shown between President Ritchie and trustee Reed Hunt, Chairman of the Board, Crown Zellerbach Corporation, who introduced Mr. Taylor for the honorary degree, Doctor of Laws.

greater satisfaction out of thanking the donor of a $10 check whom I know to have sacrificed in the giving than the donor of the $5,000 check who could much better afford it. Of course, any college president always finds very practical joy in acknowledging big checks!

Despite their best efforts to insure at least minimal privacy, the president and his family experience a rather "goldfish bowl" type of living. Although the president may own his home and may have located it away from the campus, he is still very much a part of the university scene day or night. Despite the deference which is given his position, little restraint is exercised by anybody in interrupting his sleep, his meals, his recreation, his gardening or golfing, or even his Sunday morning church hour.

One member of our faculty at Pacific for a number of years exercised the privilege of an unlisted telephone number. Although I admired his courage and was envious of the privacy it gave him and his wife, I would not have dared to follow his example. Too many calls, important and unimportant, are directed at the president's telephone for him to enjoy such a luxury. It may be a mother calling from San Francisco or Hawaii to inquire about whether her son has gotten over a bad cold. Actually, she may have failed to get the infirmary, probably didn't think of calling the dean of men or women, and just thought "she'd go to the top and get the word." In some cases the president would know about her boy, but in others he wouldn't. Had she called the dean of men he could probably have told her that the boy's cold was cured and the night before he participated in a basketball game for most of the playing time. He could also have told her that the boy tended to be careless about telephoning or writing his mother. Another reason the president would not dare have an unlisted phone is that some wealthy friend might call up and suggest that Tuesday would be the best day for the luncheon engagement concerning the caller's intention to donate to the university or provide for it in his will.

It is true that I have often complained privately about the persons who telephone at mealtime and apologize for interrupting but talk for half an hour anyway. By the time the conversation is finished the soup is cold or the dessert melted. Of course, we

53

could follow the practice of some of our friends who simply answer the telephone and say that Mr. So-and-So cannot be disturbed at his meal or when he is resting. We just never have been able to assume such an attitude of self-importance.

When the president is allowed to buy his own house on a proper allowance, he at least has the opportunity of trying to settle in a congenial community, although this is difficult because of the size and nature of the house he needs. We had been lucky in that the house we purchased in Oneonta, after the sale of the old president's house, was located in a large lot next to people who had children of their own. Consequently we became warm friends and neighbors and our children during the later years in Oneonta had perhaps the most ideal play conditions which they could have anywhere. There was a beautiful trout stream at the foot of the hill. Our son, John, spent many happy hours fishing it.

The neighbors in Forest Grove, Oregon, have been wonderful in every possible way, and our children have had a relatively normal experience so far as the neighborhood is concerned. In fact, our friends, Dr. and Mrs. Fred Richards, immediately across the street from us, have been like second parents to our youngest daughter Betsy. And Betsy's horse, Diamond, furnished free rides for the Richards' grandchildren and all the other small fry in the immediate vicinity.

Despite all this happy neighborliness, our house in Forest Grove is still something of a fishbowl. The president's house must be prepared for unexpected guests. They could be parents from Alaska or Southern California who elected to "just drop in for a brief visit." They might really be responding to a letter which the autotypewriter did at the University, the tag line being "please come to see us at the university whenever you can." For this reason the living area of the president's house must be in as tidy a condition as possible. My wife succeeds remarkably well in keeping it so, and at the same time following our determined policy of having our family use all of our house. However, when someone exclaims "how perfectly charming your house is, and it has such a nice 'lived-in' appearance," she wonders just what the latter phrase means.

At any rate, unexpected visitors do come often. One of the most unusual was a rather skinny freshman who proffered a letter and said, "I am responding to your invitation to dinner this evening." The note was purportedly from my wife inviting him to dinner at 7 o'clock. Obviously some sophomores had perpetrated this hoax, confidently expecting that at 7 o'clock we would perhaps have eaten most of our dinner and the poor freshman would be out in the cold.

I solemnly invited the young man in, kindly explained that he was the victim of a prank, but assured him that my wife would provide some dinner. We had finished eating but fortunately there was enough left to provide the young man a very adequate dinner on a tray from which he ate before the fireplace while talking to me. Indeed, he warmed to the various subjects we undertook and enjoyed his visit to the president's house so much that I finally had to remind him about 10 o'clock that I had some work to do on a speech which I was to deliver in a few days and felt he had better get along back to the men's dormitory. He left with a good story to tell the sophomores and he, the freshman, could have the last laugh!

Sometimes a guest may not be unexpected, but may stay an unexpectedly long time. One of our new administrators and his family came a little before the opening of college and we generously invited them to stay with us pending the securance of suitable quarters. We were confident these quarters could be secured shortly, but time went by and little success was had. Finally, an appropriate place was found and the couple moved in approximately three weeks after they had come to our house as guests with three lively children. Fortunately, we knew the young man and his wife very well and could make all five of the family a part of our family and no disastrous results occurred. Obviously, we all were a bit worn out at the end of the three weeks, however.

The president's house, like the minister's house, whether it is owned by the university or not, is fair game for various groups. It is often "taken over" by such groups for teas, receptions, dessert meetings and the like. Of course, the president's wife could say "no," but actually she may enjoy meeting with these groups.

Nonetheless, their frequent use of the president's house contributes to the goldfish bowl type of living for the family. It means periods of special cleanup, extra help, many people in the kitchen, sometimes outdoor luncheon tables all over the back lawn.

It is important, of course, in discussing the somewhat non-private character of the president's home life to point out that the effects are not always bad. Even the many parties, receptions and unexpected guests have some good effects. They not only perform the function of good public relations for the university, but they enable the president's family to learn to meet people of many different kinds and to be at ease with them. In our case both our daughters have learned to help with such parties whether it be waiting on tables or greeting guests at the door. In years to come both young ladies will find this experience of great value to them. Their poise with strangers has grown out of this experience to a large extent.

Of course, the goldfish bowl experience isn't confined to the home. The president and his wife must appear at the opera, the theatre on the campus and in the community if there is one, the symphony by all means, and the art shows. For Josephine and me this has been in general a great pleasure. Sometimes I attended the art shows at the university when I was too tired to see what was being shown, but the program, at least in its infancy, needed every support we could give. Since we have been at Pacific we not only attend the Pacific Community Orchestra performances, but we support the Portland Symphony. My wife attends regularly and I attend occasionally. Thus, whether we choose to do it or not we are exposed to a great deal of artistic talent and reap rich cultural benefits. Of course, it would be nice sometimes to enjoy these programs without the special feeling of obligation. That will come when we retire.

Some "must" appearances are made under most difficult conditions. In the fall of 1965 our very dear friend and trustee, John W. Pugh, retired as general secretary of the metropolitan YMCA of Portland. I was a member of the board of directors of the YMCA and, of course, knew Jack both in this capacity and in his capacity as a trustee of Pacific University. For some unaccountable reason the committee on arranging a testimonial dinner for Jack requested me to serve as master of ceremonies at the Benson Hotel.

A few days before this great occasion Josephine and I were in an automobile accident and her left ankle was badly torn and otherwise injured. What to do? I urged Josephine to stay at home and nurse the ankle, but she knew that it would be extremely awkward for me and would require explanations. So, she determined to go even though in a wheelchair.

Arrangements were made for an attendant to meet our car outside the hotel, to wheel her in, put her on an elevator and just before the proceedings began to seat her at the speakers' table with the wheelchair pushed up close to the table. Though in pain, she kept her best "first lady's smile" going throughout the entire dinner. I did have to explain why she did not rise during the invocation and thus the audience knew of the accident. I declared that she was such a great fan of Jack Pugh that she insisted on coming to his testimonial dinner even in a wheelchair. Actually, Josephine got the biggest hand of anybody except the honoree and his wife. But her strength was really quite spent when we reached Forest Grove about midnight.

Goldfish bowl living is not always pleasant and has many frustrations. It is educational. The president and his family meet the great and the near-great and many other varieties of people both in the home and in campus and community experience. Many of these people have much to offer and learning to know them is a rich experience in broadening one's own horizons.

Throughout the immediate community and often the surrounding areas the president and his wife and his entire family have social opportunities open to them that would not possibly be available if he were in some other job. Yet, unfortunately, often the social opportunities involve expense which the president and his family cannot afford. To the extent that such opportunities can be embraced, they are frequently of much value.

The eternal reminder "but you are the president," or "but you are the president's wife," or "but you are the president's son and daughter" can be exasperating. You often want to say "Why can't I just be myself?" without regard to the role. Really, I think the president and his family have a right to insist on being essentially themselves. But if they listen to the demands of the role, in its best sense, then they have to be their better selves. Perhaps there are elements in the role that would tempt them to be something else than themselves, entirely artificial selves. Of course, this demand should be rejected. If at least for most of the time the response to the role challenges them to becoming their best selves, then it is worthwhile despite frustrations and disappointments.

CHAPTER IV

Growing a Protective Shell

If college presidents, like the turtle, must stick out their necks in order to make progress, also, like the turtle, they need a good thick shell to protect them from blasts of criticism that will surely come their way. A certain college president keeps inside his desk this motto: "Count that day lost when you don't get hell for something." Robert Hutchins is reported to have said, "The administrator who cannot stand criticism, including slander and libel, is lost."

Criticism grows out of the fact that the college president is involved in decision making. And anyone who has the responsibility for final decisions or even final recommendations to a governing board is very foolish indeed if he expects to avoid criticism from persons or groups whom he may disappoint.

It is a curious thing that so crucial a job has so little professional security. In a day when college professors insist on tenure and are protected vigorously and vociferously by the American Association of University Professors, college presidents, in most cases at least, have no tenure at all. A well-known example is that of a mid-western president who went to a meeting of the board of trustees assuming that he would continue as head of the institution for many years and left the meeting dismissed from his job.

Despite the obvious onus placed on the college presidency by its insecurity, it seems to me essential that the president serve at "the pleasure of the board of trustees." He must be a mature individual with the kind of self-confidence that will enable him to work in the job which has no tenure. If he does not have this kind of self-assurance, he perhaps is not a good candidate for the presidency to begin with. If he is not strong and toughminded criticism from all quarters will certainly toughen him up, if he survives. In some respects the criticism may in fact be a measure of his success. It may be an indication of the problems with which he has to deal. It may be a valuable guide indicating the limits beyond which he cannot go. And it may be a valuable stimulus to careful analysis which will bring the institution to greater days. Whatever its value or lack of value, criticism will be relatively constant. A successful president is sensitive enough to respond to it profitably.

Since the beginning of universities students have been critical of their superiors. In more recent years the conflict between students and administration has been accentuated. In the small college, student demonstrations may be less frequent than in large universities, but student criticism is often more pointed and more personal.

Only a few months after my becoming president of Hartwick, Norman Roper, the business manager, told me that the college must borrow money for the payroll. His explanation was that the students' bills had not been collected and that they were permitted to wait until the end of the semester to pay. In the meantime the college had to borrow payroll money.

I was astonished at this practice and immediately gave instructions that students would be required to pay their second semester bills immediately or to make arrangements for loans which would provide the money for the college. Students were furious at the rash action of the new president. One blonde youngster charged me with being "un-Christian." He said to me: "If you insist on my paying my bills to the college, I will be unable to pay my fraternity bills and will have to drop out." And then he added mournfully, "In fact, I may even have to sell my car."

My tart reply was: "Young man, if you can afford the twin luxuries of a fraternity and an automobile, you can pay your college bills—or you can go home."

Perhaps the other most violent criticism during the six years at Hartwick had to do with fraternity housemothers. When we arrived we heard all kinds of stories about the rowdy parties thrown by fraternities. Although we naturally discounted the stories, investigation showed that they had some foundation in fact. Furthermore, on our visits to fraternity dinners we noted that the boys were almost completely bereft of any knowledge of entertaining. The food was terrible and the service was worse. The students insistently asked for visiting privileges for girls which we could not grant.

Another bad situation had to do with cost. The college had only slightly over 300 students, not enough to furnish applications for the four fraternities. Consequently the groups sought to "sell" membership by lowering the rates for room and board below those of the college dormitory.

In order to remedy the situation, I asked for and got a resolution by the board of trustees requiring that fraternities charge for room and board at least as much as the college charged and requiring that by a certain date fraternities should provide appropriate quarters and should hire housemothers.

Several kinds of hell broke loose at once. Yellow sheets were distributed all over the campus accusing me of being a dictator with language such as the following:

"The SHOCKING and Dictatorial Proclamation of President Ritchie is a grave threat to the rights of Hartwick Students and shows complete scorn for the Student Government and for the principles of Democracy itself. The Ultimate Power in Government, said John Locke, is LAW WITHIN COMMON CONSENT. Not only does this threaten to reduce Fraternities and Sororities to mere puppet organizations but paves the way for the complete subjection of ALL students. Ritchie has already stated that he is against automobiles on Campus. What next? Hours for men? White shirts and ties in class?

How can we fight this? Although President Ritchie seems to have made it clear that he will not be influenced by the student government bodies, we can give the existing democratic machinery a fair trial.

However, if this fails, the only logical recourse is REVOLT."

Another posed a threatening question: "Wouldn't next year's supposedly large? Frosh Class like to be informed of this last militant order. How fast would H. C. grow." Anonymous calls

61

flooded our telephone including the admonition "go home, Southerner."

After several days a delegation of fraternity boys appeared in my office and the spokesman laid down the challenge as follows: "Mr. President, you have only about 300 students here now. Every fraternity man on the campus will leave unless you reverse the action. When we do this, just what shape will you and Hartwick College be in?"

I had no time to think through an answer and there was really little choice. I said: "Gentlemen, if you will give me a list of all fraternity men who expect to leave, your academic transcripts will be ready by tomorrow afternoon so that you can transfer to some other institution. Good day."

Though I was pretty well shaken by the threat, it turned out to be a bluff. As I recall it, not a single student transferred. About a year later a reception was held under my wife's leadership, with the housemothers and the presidents of each fraternity in the receiving line. The boys were all dressed up and so were the housemothers. Afterwards, I am sure, had we insisted on eliminating the housemothers, the students would have revolted with equal fervor. With good housemothers, entertaining improved, order came into fraternal lives and, best of all, the brothers could have young lady visitors in the fraternity houses with proper chaperonage.

In the fraternity situation one student earned my very great respect by writing me the most bitterly critical letter I have ever received. Among other things he said: "A man who speaks in one breath about the 'cooperation and fellowship of the student,' and then stabs the student in the back with the next breath, certainly commands no respect from me, or from any of my fellow students. . . . I have no complaint against the faculty of this institution, they have done a thorough job, in preparing me for my career. But an institution with an administration like this one, is no institution at all. . . . If this sort of policy continues, I can see Hartwick in five more years. Oh, it will have its beautiful campus, and the President's porch light may be on, but it will lack one thing. When the professors come to their eight o'clock lectures some morning, they may find something missing, THE

STUDENTS! I suggest that you and the 'Bored of Trustees,'* think this matter over, very carefully. It looks like you may have a full-scale revolt on your hands. . . . (*Not misspelled, most of them are.)"

The reason I admired this young man is that he had the courage to sign his name. Undoubtedly he expected that I would expel him. Actually I took no disciplinary action whatever and took considerable pleasure in handing him his diploma when he graduated. I trust he is providing distinguished leadership in some field of professional or business endeavor now. I also like to think that he speaks with considerable understanding of the "fraternity crisis" at Hartwick. Perhaps he even has told his son of the values of having housemothers in fraternity houses.

At Pacific University, the greatest student uproar became known as the "Necktie Rebellion." It occurred in our second year at Pacific and was an interesting example of student group reaction to supposed "foreign" standards. The changes which precipitated the "rebellion" arose out of great concern on my part for the way in which the University was unintentionally "shortchanging" the students.

Shortly after Josephine and I arrived we visited the cafeteria on the ground floor of McCormick Hall. We noted with considerable astonishment the fact that the students were taking their meals in what appeared to be Army surplus trays—no dishes. We were terribly embarrassed not only by the sloppy serving of the food, but by the equally sloppy appearance of the students. They wore anything they desired, including the sloppiest kind of sweaters, sweat-shirts and other kinds of gear. Students would sit with their feet draped over chairs and even on the tables. Waste of food was rampant. The whole atmosphere was a matter of "feeding" rather than dining.

I determined that the following year, regardless of cost, we would provide good-quality hotel dishes, making necessary the purchase of a large and expensive new dishwashing arrangement. But something had to be done to improve the behavior of the students. Under the leadership of the Dean of Students, Bryce Dunham, the matter was discussed by an appropriate committee. Although I did not take direct leadership I certainly had a strong directive influence. The result was a new ruling to the effect that young ladies would wear suitable dresses and footgear, and men students would wear coats and ties to dinner each day.

The announcement was made during the summer months. As soon as the University opened in the fall trouble began. The students were vociferous in their criticism, and they immediately heaped the blame on the president and his wife. We were accused of importing "eastern ideas." It never occurred to the students to notice with appreciation the new dishes and the much improved service in the Commons, including a new hostess, Mrs. Elace Loper. The men students were especially vociferous in declaring that they could not afford to wear coats and ties.

A number of the men students came to see me, using the expense factor as their argument. With my wife's cooperation I provided a novel answer. I would reach in the lefthand corner of my desk drawer and pull out a handful of neckties she had selected from my tie rack at home. I would generously offer one of these ties to the complaining student. Perhaps it was my conservative taste or the student's pride, but there were no takers. Nonetheless, my offer eliminated the necktie expense argument.

Students claimed that the administration was trying to revolutionize their manners and that in their hometowns people did not wear coats and ties. I would quietly ask whether they expected to return to their hometowns, to take up their profession or business. Almost invariably the answer was, "No, I expect to work in Denver, San Francisco, Seattle, Portland, or some other large city." Then I invited them to go to Portland and check on the number of people who go even to lunch at the better hotels or clubs without coats and ties. And I added the comment that Pacific University was not interested in graduating the fourth assistant to the assistant to the vice president of the business firm, but was interested in graduating the boy who had the capabilities and the leadership to be vice president or president of the firm. In this case he would most likely need to be accustomed to wearing coat and tie, at least to dinner.

To enforce the "coat and tie rule" at the dinner hour we provided a resolute young man as a checker on the serving line. Anybody who was not properly dressed was told to come back later. Reports came to me of very ingenious attires tried by the students, including one enterprising youth who appeared in a bedsheet with a laurel wreath adorning his brow, and two co-eds with brooms who swept a royal path preceding him to the Commons. Another appeared in swim trunks, track shoes and a tie with the ends sliced off dangling below his Adam's apple. The student bouncer did his stuff, however, and the pranks gradually subsided.

The administration simply held firm in the matter and as time went on the students became accustomed to the new standards and, as one housemother who ate regularly in the Commons remarked, the general conduct in the Commons "improved about 90%." In fact, some of the students began to feel a real sense of pride, as visiting speakers and visiting groups who dined in the Commons complimented them on their fine appearance.[1]

Ironically, one of the most innocent of those who "stay up" the president's hands received some of the strongest criticism. Some of the students generously gave my wife, Josephine, credit for master-minding the whole affair as well as having influence toward stricter dormitory rules. Those who had been in our home obviously related the traditional furniture and some of the more or less formal dinners and receptions we gave to "eastern customs."

Actually, Josephine had nothing directly to do with the situation, although her taste and her influence undoubtedly had affected me through the years. But then students do not observe such fine distinctions. Bryce Dunham, the dean of students, early one morning spied an effigy hanging from a tree nearby the women's dormitory. On it, among other things, were the words, "Deliver us from the moral Mrs. Ritchie." Bryce cut it down, brought it to my office and I hastily placed it in the back end of my closet. Later I destroyed it, having taken the various uncomplimentary placards off it.

I was very fearful that Josephine would be heartbroken by her

---

[1] In more recent years the "coat and tie" rule has been liberalized for various reasons. One special reason is the difficulty in applying specific criteria in a period in which accepted styles have such variety. Nowadays students are asked to dress for "special" dinners.

involuntary induction into the "exclusive Pacific University effigy society." However, I knew that I would have to tell her and screwed up my courage to do so. Much to my surprise and delight, she smiled wryly and said: "Well, if the students are going to call me anything, I'm glad they called me 'the moral Mrs Ritchie.'" To this day she has never shown any signs of resentment or bitterness respecting the episode. But it did show that one of the elements of risk for a dedicated college first lady can be that of being "hanged in effigy" by some foolish, misguided students. The Pacific University Effigy Society includes the dean of students, the business manager and the dean of the University during my time. So far I have escaped.

I have increasingly come to have a keen appreciation of the role of the student newspaper in respect to criticism. Many years before I became a college president I was a faculty adviser to a student publication. But, when you are president or dean, the point of view changes quite a bit, although the previous experience is of tremendous value. At Hartwick College, shortly before I was inaugurated, an episode occurred which grew out of a sincere but completely misdirected editorial splurge by a student editor.

I was astonished on opening the student newspaper about a week before my inauguration to read the following:

> "Hartwick College has finally been blessed with a capable, efficient, future-minded president. In welcoming him, we take cognizance of the administrative ash heap he has inherited, and our sincere pity is his. Hartwick College has, in the past few years, slithered down the drain of incompetence, at times with speeds that were incredible. It has developed a sour student body, a lethargic Alumni Association, and an overtired, overworked faculty. People have not been happy here; something has been missing—an indefinable something that is displayed in school spirit, cooperation, eagerness, and collegiate traditions. We that have had the misfortune to witness this decay, and to smell the stench, feel that at last we have a firm grip on the edge of the manhole—we can look over the edge and see the hand reaching towards us to haul us out of the morass."

Obviously the editor, Bob Vidulich, thought he was supporting the new administration by blasting the old. Of course, he could not possibly have done a more negative thing. I quickly made a statement to the local newspaper as follows:

> "The Hilltops editorial containing negative criticism of the previous administration was a shocking surprise to me and is a source of deep regret.
>
> "Every day, as I become better acquainted with the problems and achievements of Hartwick College, I have a deeper appreciation of the untiring efforts of my predecessor (Arnold).
>
> "His devotion to the college is a constant source of inspiration to me. I am sure that all who love the college, regardless of whether they agreed with the previous administrative policies, have a deep sense of gratitude to this intrepid Hartwick pioneer."

I then called the young man in and had a long conference with him on responsible journalism. He apologized to Dr. Arnold, tried to redress the situation in every possible way, and then provided us with an excellent newspaper send-off when the inauguration took place. Each person who attended the inauguration was presented a copy of "Hilltops" as he left.

Had I been wiser, I would have had a conference along policy lines with the young man considerably in advance of the time this happened. His criticism was entirely overdrawn through lack of understanding of the hardships and the problems of my predecessor and his contrasting praise of a new, relatively unproved administration, was entirely previous and in poor taste. But I'm glad I did not expel him. He is now Dr. Robert N. Vidulich, a distinguished professor of psychology in a major university. In fact, I have unsuccessfully tried to hire him.

Shortly after I came to Pacific University, a somewhat similar occasion occurred in which the student newspaper blasted the administration roundly for disregarding scheduling practices on the campus. Actually the president's office had nothing whatever to do with the so-called violations of scheduling practices. But knowing that any disavowal of responsibility would call for some indication of where it should lie with resultant repeat blastings of the so-called guilty parties, I quietly kept my counsel, took the criticism, and let it wear off in good time.

On another occasion the college newspaper strongly criticized the administration, meaning the president, for not having directly informed the students and the parents of a tuition increase before it was announced in the papers. Actually, the increase was announced as the result of a trustees' meeting and in the absence of an appropriate opportunity to publish it in the school newspaper. The fault was mine in that I could have arranged the matter otherwise, and this I frankly admitted to the editor of the school newspaper. The next time tuition was increased I sent out the notices ahead of time and released the story simultaneously to the school paper and to the local and area press.

Experiences such as this have led me to develop the practice of having an off-the-record conference with the new editor of the college newspaper. I tried to fill him or her in as honestly as possible with all predictable future events which can be discussed. The conference is strictly off the record and the information is for background so that he will know why things happen when they happen. Usually this technique has an excellent effect in establishing mutual confidence and in stimulating the editor to check with the president's office for accuracy of stories.

Within the last few years I have begun the practice of having a "fourth estate" luncheon or dinner. I invite to it the editors and business managers of the college newspaper, the literary magazine, the student year book, and the program director and business manager of the campus radio station. In addition I invite the director of public information, who edits Pacific Today, a general university magazine incorporating alumni emphasis. These meetings have been most enthusiastically received by the students.

In every possible way I make myself available to the student press and cooperate in coverage of university activities. I carefully avoid caustic criticism of the college newspaper and other publications except where gross inaccuracies occur. Then I do not hesitate to see that the record is corrected. For many years at Pacific we have had a fine reputation for free student journalism. This the students seem to appreciate and from time to time even acknowledge in editorials. This does not mean that the university would not intervene if the student press became wholly irresponsible. But as long as it is responsible, we believe in recognizing its freedom.

College faculty members have been described as "those who think otherwise." A teaching faculty member myself in former years, I have done my share of "thinking otherwise." No college president in his right mind would ever want a rubber stamp faculty. A vigorous, intellectual ferment is the heartbeat of higher education. And certainly if this be true both the Hartwick College and the Pacific University campuses during my leadership have been very healthy places.

At Hartwick I recall one professor with whom I frequently had differences of opinion. One morning I entered the administration building, Bresee Hall, and greeted him with "It's a fine morning." Without batting an eye he gave back, "Yes, that's one thing we agree on." Another professor, now deceased, was reported to be very critical of my ideas on liberal education. One informant told me of a particularly acid attack, and expressed the opinion that I should do something about it. In reply I asked him, "Did he attack the college?" The answer: "No, he just attacked you, said you know nothing about liberal education." My answer: "That's fine. So long as he stays busy attacking me he will not get around to attacking the college. I shall let him strictly alone." Of course, there were many other reports of criticisms by faculty at Hartwick, some of them undoubtedly sheer rumor by the time they reached us. In general, however, faculty members were most cooperative, very loyal and hard-working.

At Pacific University I have been fortunate in having good cooperation from the faculty. Undoubtedly there has been criticism as on every campus, but so far there has been no hint of the kind of revolt that was a causal factor in the termination of the leadership of one of my distinguished predecessors, Dr. Walter Giersbach. He and his faculty came to a parting of the ways after he had been president nearly twelve years. However, since that time the faculty of the University have voted unanimously to confer upon him the Doctor of Laws degree and he has participated together with my other predecessor, Dr. Charles Arm-

69

strong, in a Founders Day program. Dr. Armstrong was also awarded an honorary doctorate.

One episode occurred within my years at Pacific that sounded very ugly as portrayed in the Portland Reporter. The headlines read "Ten Faculty Members Resign at Pacific University." The newspaper further intimated that this apparent mass resignation took place because a certain professor was leaving the University and for other reasons of dissatisfaction. Actually, two professors, to my best knowledge, left the University because they shared the dissatisfied professor's peeve over his not receiving a promotion that particular year and over a disagreement on certain policies respecting his department. The other young professors were either going on sabbatical, going on to graduate school, or taking very attractive jobs. The situation with respect to the changes had been known throughout the year and, with the exceptions noted, had nothing directly to do with the disgruntled professor's situation.

The newspaper made it appear that the students were ready to rebel and that there would be a large exodus of students. None of this was true. Yet the big headlines continued for a week or more, including an editorial condemning me for "poor administration" and describing my work in very unflattering terms. Fortunately for the University, the more responsible newspapers in Portland, the Journal and the Oregonian, treated the episode without sensationalism. My statements were given fair emphasis and the story was kept in sensible balance.

Throughout the whole episode I refused to fight back in like manner and continued to describe the person in question as an "excellent professor." In fact, to this day I deeply regret his leaving the University so far as his teaching ability was concerned. However, his attitude seemed to me to be immature in that he had just been on a sabbatical at the expense of the University, had a very light teaching load, was not overworked on committees, and would most surely have been promoted the following year along with two other professors contemporary with him.

At any rate, the tempest in the teapot finally subsided, without riots, without any great exodus, and with excellent new faculty coming in. Not too long thereafter I was in San Francisco and saw a newspaper headline to the effect that the Portland Reporter had finally ceased to publish and was completely defunct. I must confess that for a few moments I had an evil feeling of elation. Of course, I quickly replaced it with appropriate feelings of regret that a publication with potential for useful journalistic expression had died in early childhood.

I am thankful that the faculty at Pacific University are very frank in their criticism when they feel disposed to be critical. Shortly after he came here one of our professors vehemently criticized me to my face in a committee meeting. It grew out of the fact that the president of the University is automatically a member of all University committees. I was participating in a committee meeting in this role. It was in order for me to express an opinion on a particular item that I said in effect: "As president of the University, I would have to take such and such a position."

This triggered the criticism. The professor in question reminded me as though I were an elementary school child that on committees I was not president of the University and should not try to behave as such. He went on at a great rate much to my embarrassment and that of other members of the committee. I was really too stunned to say anything except to make the point that members of the faculty and administration in a small university cannot have such neat distinctions, and that the president can never really cease being president. This is almost literally true, even when he is at home. Afterwards several of the professors apologized on behalf of the vehement faculty member. I'm sure it was expected that I would take some forceful action, but I simply let it pass.

Later the same professor did really stir my ire and hurt my administrative feelings when he opposed my soliciting faculty contributions to the new library fund. And I was equally astonished that certain others of the faculty joined him in this. Although I didn't make a big fuss about the matter, I still cannot see how members of a faculty could possibly object to being asked to contribute to so important an instrument of instruction as a library. However, I didn't consider the amount of money derived from faculty solicitation sufficient to risk a "revolution" and let the matter pass.

It isn't always the faculty members who are critical. Sometimes it's the faculty ladies. When the location for the University Center was chosen and it became known that construction would necessitate the moving of Old College Hall (1850) and the cutting down of several trees, I received a protesting letter from the secretary of the Faculty Women's Club as follows:

> "It has been extremely disconcerting to our membership to learn of the proposed building plans for the library and the student union building. We feel the desecration of the most cherished area of the campus, that involving Birch Grove and Old College Hall, may prove even more upsetting to alumni and friends of the college.

> "It is possible that architects have decided conclusively that there is no alternative; but it seems to our members that the more unattractive areas of our campus, such as those fronting Pacific Avenue, might better be utilized first. We find it difficult to believe that healthy young girls could not walk a block to a dining hall."

Fortunately, this did not get into the newspapers. I immediately arranged to speak to the Faculty Women's Club and took the architect with me. We arranged to have a model of the million-dollar new University Center building there, together with the plans. I also carried with me extensive data from the Ford Foundation Educational Facilities Center. The architect and I explained as patiently as possible the rather complicated process of campus planning and building location. I quoted liberally from the Ford Facilities Center data and described how the new building was located exactly where the experts say a university center should be on a campus.

The architect and I covered every imaginable point and went into the subject with considerable depth. We then asked for questions and insisted that we wanted to answer every possible question anybody might be willing to voice. The result was we really wore the subject threadbare, and the ladies seemed to be completely satisfied. At least that was the last we heard of strong criticism from this particular quarter.

72

I have made it a rigid rule to try to attend every meeting of the Faculty Council except when some emergency requires my absence. This keeps me in close touch with faculty leadership and enables me to have candid exchanges with the members of the Council. We don't always agree. Sometimes we get a bit heated, but at least we understand each other and communicate effectively. Of course, there is the monthly faculty meeting, but this is more formalized and is never as effective an instrument of communication, however valuable it may be in bringing the entire faculty group together.

Since the construction of our new University Center with its excellent coffee shop, I have made it a practice to drop in immediately after I pick up my mail and sit down at one of the coffee tables with the professors who happen to be there. Five minutes sitting beside a young professor enables me to have brief conversation with him. Often there is a general group discussion in which I participate briefly.

A college community is much larger than the students, faculty and administration. It includes the trustees, the alumni, the related church if there is one, parents of students, and certainly friends who have invested their interest, their effort and their treasure in the college. Often from these quarters come stinging criticism of the president and sometimes other leaders of the college.

One of our trustees at Hartwick, now deceased, gave me a real going-over concerning an honorary degree for the then Attorney General of New York, Jacob Javits. The honorary degree committee on which this trustee sat had unanimously approved the LL.D. degree for Mr. Javits. But an emergency legal matter prevented his being present at the scheduled time, Founders Day, in October. His assistant telephoned me and asked whether it could be conferred at a later time. I agreed and scheduled it for the spring commencement.

Word got to the critical trustee that the conferral time had been changed and he jumped to the conclusion that Mr. Javits had insulted the college. Together with several other trustees whom he had influenced he came to me and in the most rugged language condemned Mr. Javits and demanded that the degree be cancelled. Although I had great respect and affection for the trustee, I felt he was entirely out of order and told him so. I held that the approving of the conferral was the business of the committee and managing the timing of the conferral was the business of the administration. Further, I held that Mr. Javits' reasons were perfectly legitimate.

The following June Jacob Javits served as commencement speaker and delivered a statesmanlike address. It was my great pleasure to confer upon him the Doctor of Laws degree. Shortly after that he was elected United States senator and has served with distinction in that capacity. As it turned out the degree for Jacob Javits was one of the more popular degrees conferred. Through the years he has been a friend of Hartwick College and a friend of mine.

Sometimes the administrative leader must demand recognition of his rights and responsibilities. Another episode from Hartwick days illustrating this point was a visit I had from an alumni committee of a fraternity. The fraternity in question had just been put on probation which meant that the members could not attend social functions. The alumni committee demanded that this ban be lifted temporarily so that the members of the fraternity could attend the annual alumni dance to be held in the community.

I flatly told the committee that I felt their concern should be cooperation with the University in seeing that the errant group of young men conformed to regulations. The committee implied various kinds of reprisals such as withdrawing support, refusing to recommend students and general non-cooperation with the college. I expressed regret but stood my ground. To my knowledge the episode caused very little harm to the college. Shortly thereafter I was visited by an alumni committee from another fraternity. This time, however, the committee came asking how it might cooperate with the college in encouraging the boys on probation to meet the requirements of the college and to get back into the good graces of the dean of students. I gladly gave advice and referred the committee to the dean of students and promised to instruct him to cooperate in every possible way. The result was a most happy one and both the college and the fraternity benefited.

Sometimes alumni take other tactics. At one of the fall conferences at Pacific University I addressed the faculty on the subject, "Winds of Change in Higher Education." In the course of the talk I spoke of developments such as the trimester system, of the need to modernize the approach to space, time, personnel use, and various other recent developments in higher education. Along the way I took rather deadly aim at certain campus sacred cows. My speech was reported in the Portland papers very accurately although the juiciest parts were used without the balancing effects of qualifying statements. Within a few days I received an anonymous postcard which accused me of seeking publicity with a lot of wild ideas and threatened to organize the alumni, march on Forest Grove, and get me out! It was signed "an alumnus."

Sometimes a president "catches it" from leaders in the supporting church. At Hartwick College shortly after my inauguration I received a rude shock in the form of a letter from one of the ministers from the supporting church. He castigated me for having a person of doubtful religious persuasion speak at the inauguration, alleged that we had not shown proper respect to the church relationship, and generally accused me of staging a heathen ceremony at a church-related college. Furthermore, he forwarded a copy of his letter to the national president of the supporting church. Obviously, this could result in getting me fired and in destroying the little college that seemed on the verge of financial extinction anyhow. However fallible I might be, at that particular juncture I was very necessary to the life of the institution. Actually, the speaker objected to was Dr. Everett Clinchy, president of the National Conference of Christians and Jews, and an ordained Presbyterian minister. My inaugural address contained appropriate references to the supporting church, and the inauguration had all necessary and appropriate religious emphasis.

Hurt and angry, I immediately wrote a letter giving the lie to the critic and sent copies to all trustees and to the president of the supporting church. Reassuring letters poured in from the trustees. The president of the church assured me that he did not share the highly critical feelings of my correspondent. Later I learned that the man was quite sincere though misguided. He

75

learned that I was also sincere, though he undoubtedly continued to feel that my "liberal" religious attitude was suspect.

Sometimes a prospective or active donor will be critical. While at Hartwick I served as chairman of the local Brotherhood Council, an affiliate of the National Conference of Christians and Jews. I had been active in this great national organization for a number of years and had occupied a professorship at the University of Miami endowed by a great leader in the National Conference. One year the national office of the Council recognized the brotherhood week programming of the local Council by a special award that was received at a great banquet meeting with the president of the Chamber of Commerce on hand as well as officers of the local round table. Everybody in town was happy that the small city of Oneonta had been singled out for special recognition.

Within the next couple of years, however, our Psychology Department did a survey of the community and found that in the community at large there was just about as much expression of feelings of prejudice as in the average American community. When this research report was published in the local newspaper, our director of development came rushing into my office showing evidence of great concern. He said that a very wealthy man in the community had taken serious offense at the research and felt that I should have suppressed it. I tried to quell his fears as well as make very clear that the college would not suppress honest research. As it turned out, the critic cooled off and continued a strong and loyal friend of the college.

There are always possibilities of criticism. If the president stays on campus too much, he is criticized for not being out raising funds. If he is out raising funds constantly, the faculty criticizes him for caring nothing about the academic process. If his pictures appear in the paper too much he is reported to be a publicity hound; if they appear too little he is said to be a man of no consequence in the community and derelict in his duty to represent the college. A president simply cannot win the battle of criticism. He must be willing to take it.

Perhaps the most obnoxious vehicle for criticism is the anonymous telephone call. During our six years at Hartwick College we were bedeviled from time to time with such calls. Occasionally it was the garbled voice of a student who had been drinking excessively and undoubtedly had been dared to call the president's telephone number and wake him up. Others were much more serious. The prize one in our memory, however, is the call that came in the middle of the night, after I had returned from an extended speaking trip. Josephine quickly answered and I slept on. The voice vehemently described the terrible antics of a group of young "hoodlums" at one of our dormitories, a former hospital, in the town at the foot of the hillside campus.

My wife said in surprise, "Why these are not hoodlums. They are a group of church youth here for a conference. They are occupying the dormitory for a couple of nights." Then the caller demanded to talk to "that bird Ritchie." My wife lost her temper and said, "My husband is not a bird, and he has just come from a very exhausting speaking trip and I will not call him unless you identify yourself and speak in a courteous manner." That did it. The caller hung up. The next morning Josephine informed me of the episode through which I had slept peacefully. I puzzled over it a bit and then said, "But how could this be? Before I left we arranged to have faculty chaperones in the dormitory and certainly this kind of rumpus could not have taken place. I must check into this when I get to the campus."

When I reached the campus I called in Dr. Wallace Klinger, the dean of the college who was the director of the summer session. I described the situation to Wallace and said, "Who the dickens were the chaperones in this dormitory?" Wallace Klinger's face broke into a mischievous smile and he said, "Hilda (his wife) and I were the chaperones!" And then he explained that one of the buses bringing the young people had been delayed and had arrived in the middle of the night. Naturally the youngsters had made noise as they unloaded the bus and occupied the dormitory. Obviously, this was normal and the complaining telephone caller had simply been bothered in his sleep and so had been devoid of understanding of how teenagers normally react. Dean Klinger and I often told the story, however, to illustrate that even with the dean and his wife as chaperones, youngsters could be called "hoodlums."

One of the most un-Christian letters of criticism I ever received at Hartwick came from an anonymous person who protested the fact that our church-related college had accepted for admission a young man whose mother was a "low woman . . . with no good reputation." She described the alleged activities of his mother, opined that he would infect the college with evil and generally identified us as on the way to hell because of this departure from what she considered appropriate behavior for religiously affiliated institutions. Actually, the boy was a fine young man who had a good high school record and deserved much more than most youngsters a chance in life. I keep the letter to this day just to illustrate how "un-Christian" some so-called Christian people can be.

At Pacific there have been far less anonymous telephone calls than at Hartwick. Maybe it is the difference between East and West. But from time to time there has been some very interesting mail. In 1960 I received the Melby Award for leadership in human relations from New York University where years before I had taken advanced studies. The Award was presented at a large alumni convocation in the new Loeb Center on Washington Square. Scarcely had I gotten home to Oregon before a letter appeared in my mail on very "crackly," expensive-appearing stationery. It warned me of the dire communist implications in the award and of the dangerous "liberal" tendencies of Dr. Melby. It even alleged that Dr. Melby was seeking to make inroads in Oregon by arranging for me to have this award.

To the credit of the writer, he signed his name. I wrote him a courteous response, explaining to him that the award was not made by Dr. Melby, dean emeritus of the School of Education, but by the alumni of the school; that Dr. Melby was then distinguished professor of education at the University of Michigan; and that he would be welcome at any time on the Pacific University campus but that I did not think the University could afford his lecture fees at the time. I am quite sure the letter did not satisfy the critic, but it did set the record straight.

Another choice number in my special file is a letter from a lady who puts college dramatic productions in strange company. Our theatre group at Pacific University had done *The Beggar's*

78

Opera, much to the delight of all who attended. But scarcely had the last applause died away before a letter came from a woman in a small Oregon community addressed to me. It upbraided the college for allowing such a production and asked, "Who runs the training of your students? The Reds? Well, it looks like it." After exhausting this subject the writer launched into a discussion of fluoridation of the water as a Communist plot. According to the logic of the letter, the very innocent act of allowing the production of The Beggar's Opera indicated the college was for fluoridation of the water and by virtue of being for fluoridation of the water Pacific was surely a fellow-traveler or possibly a real communist institution.

Of course this letter, along with many others, went into what I call "The Nut File." Every president must have such a file. In my file there are all kinds of crackpot-attack letters and other strange communications. One of them is from a chap who announces himself as Jesus Christ. Others have various plans to save the world. Of course, a good many are simply thrown into the waste basket and not filed. Being interested in "characters," whether they appear in letters or appear in other forms, I have kept a number of samples.

Every campus abounds with critical rumors. Even as we were preparing to leave Oneonta, New York, with innumerable expressions of good will, a bit overweight from the wonderful farewell dinners, and warmed by the praise and appreciation of the trustees, we heard the rumor that the real reason I was going to Pacific University was that I was receiving a $40,000 salary. I did ask the Pacific University trustees for a substantial salary which they gladly agreed to, but it certainly wasn't within a mile of $40,000. As has been said, our overriding motivating factor was locating in a good climate for our daughter Betsy whose health was extremely delicate at the time. As a matter of fact, my successor at Hartwick, I strongly suspect, made a much larger salary than I am receiving at present. And he was provided a magnificent president's house, formerly the home of a trustee. My successor deserved both the salary and the home, for the college prospered under his direction and responded to his leadership.

Here in Oregon one of the state colleges lost its president

several years ago. In the course of a few weeks my wife heard the rumor in Forest Grove that I was on the verge of accepting the presidency. The fact was that the college did not approach me and had it done so I would have refused. At various points is one's career as the president of a college, he returns from a few days out of town only to find his mission has been entirely misconstrued. Sometimes he learns to his complete astonishment that he has found enough money to endow the institution forever, or that he has been offered a fabulous opportunity in another state, or even more far-fetched that he has been "living it up" in some "fleshpot" city such as San Francisco, New Orleans, Miami, Chicago, or New York. Many interesting and unexpected things happen to a college president. Sometimes the criticism is not only unexpected but is also interesting. The college president who can accept it, sometimes laugh about it and at bedtime forget it and sleep soundly, is most likely to endure if not succeed.

CHAPTER V

Negro-White Marriage: Test of Campus Maturity

Discussions of racial integration on the American campus almost invariably raise the question of courtship and marriage. Especially is this true regarding Negro and white students.

The stock answers are that students of different races really aren't interested in marriage to each other; that the probability is greatly overstressed; that the number of such marriages is statistically insignificant; that people these days are too sophisticated to get upset about it; and that we won't have to face the situation on our campus.

But this syrupy response to the question, though partly true, is not really honest. I found this out within very soon after beginning my first college presidency.

The man who walked into my office in August, 1953, was pale, obviously agitated, and deeply troubled. As I recall it, his words were something to this effect, coming in jerky sentences, painfully spoken: "We must stop this terrible thing from happening!"

"What terrible thing is it?" I asked.

"A Negro-white marriage. And the girl is my daughter!"

The man was Harold Rushmore, a prominent attorney in a small upstate New York town. The boy was Douglas Jones and the girl was Barbara Rushmore, both students at Hartwick College where I had become the President a few short weeks before. I had heard vaguely about a courtship between a Negro student and a white student, but had been so preoccupied with

81

the financial crisis which threatened the life of the college as I began my work that I paid little attention.

Mr. Rushmore's presence in my office made it abundantly clear that it was not just a casual courtship and that it had in it the makings of a social crisis that might seriously threaten the little college of approximately 300 students. Hartwick was almost totally bereft of confidence in the town of Oneonta at the time, and had a monstrous pile of bills and debts which threatened its very existence. The situation could destroy the college and send me into professional oblivion.

There flashed across my mind a statement of my friend Dr. Dan Dodson, professor of Educational Sociology at New York University and formerly executive director of the Mayor's Committee on Unity in New York City. I had counseled with him about accepting the presidency of the college, leaving the chairmanship of the Human Relations Department at the University of Miami where I was involved in the study of race relations problems in the South. Dan had said: "Don't feel guilty about leaving the South, Miller, you will face some human relations problems in New York State."

Another thought—a question—hit me full force as I looked into the perplexed face of the father. What is the Christian commitment of the college in this situation? Hartwick proudly emphasized its admission of all applicants without regard to race or creed or ethnic background. And of course, as a former professor of Human Relations I subscribed to this idea. Here was a totally unexpected and real-life test of this commitment, personal and professional.

But at the moment I had a greatly disturbed father in my office and he was demanding answers. "Mr. Rushmore," I said, "I have scarcely arrived on this campus which is full of problems, and I know practically nothing about this situation."

He responded apologetically, "I'm sorry to upset you, but I must have help. Up to now we have just not been able to break up the relationship."

This was a cue to talk some sense to him.

"Mr. Rushmore, in most courtships, regardless of race, efforts

82

to separate the young people frequently achieve just the opposite effect."

Obviously, this statement shook him, but he replied, "But we have to do something, my daughter simply must not marry a Negro and be dragged down to his inferior racial level!"

I know my next comment was in a way academic, but it helped: "Mr. Rushmore, there are no superior races. There are only superior individuals, and they are members of all races. Of course, there are advanced and backward cultures and groups within cultures, and there are people who reflect this fact."

He shot back at me, "You sound like you are for such a marriage!"

"Frankly, Mr. Rushmore, I am just for good marriages. This I am sure of. In this case I couldn't possibly have an opinion, for I don't even know the young people involved. Of course, I am not against it in line with the racist arguments. Notions of mongrelization and weakening the racial strain have been pretty well disproved by the anthropologists.

"The real problem in this or any other Negro-white marriage is the social prejudice and discrimination that exists. The chances for success in such a marriage, according to usual standards, are very limited.

"My advice to you is to talk with the boy and the girl quietly about the difficulties they face and to base your objections upon the social facts rather than upon the cliches of prejudice that are not only invalid but would be wholly unacceptable to the young couple. In the final analysis it will have to be their decision as to whether they want to take the risk of success or failure in the face of the social taboos that still remain in our society respecting Negro-white marriages."

As Mr. Rushmore left, I felt that our discussion had served a useful purpose in providing a release of tension and of getting some of the elements of the problem out where they could be analyzed with some intelligence. The very fact that I did not express sympathy for his view stemming from prejudice and his unfounded fears seemed to be helpful. But it was obvious I had not allayed his fears, and indeed, they could not be allayed.

Although I had great sympathy for the bewildered father and

undoubtedly his equally bewildered wife, I was perhaps even more concerned about the effect upon the college campus.

My secretary notified the deans of the college and the personnel deans to meet with me immediately. Before they arrived, however, I came to two fixed conclusions: 1) The college must live up to its moral commitment respecting the rights of individuals; it could not admit students of all races and then be party to discriminating against them after they were admitted. 2) Every effort must be made to avoid Hartwick's becoming the center of a racial controversy.

When the deans assembled in my office, I mentioned Mr. Rushmore's visit. Then I asked them about the young couple and their status in the college. In the discussion it seemed clear to me that expressions of disapproval from one quarter or another in the college had been made. On the other hand, it was clearly established that no rights or privileges had been denied the young couple.

When I went home for dinner that evening, my wife knew I was worried. She can always tell. Later in the evening I told her the story. With some bitterness I said: "The easy way out would be simply to eliminate the kids from college. And curiously enough, that is exactly what a lot of folks would expect a president who is a native Southerner to do.

"Little did I think we would be facing such a race relations problem as this, almost before we got settled in upstate New York. And it just seems to me that our whole intellectual and religious commitment may be at stake. Obviously, we must stand by what we believe in, but who knows what this will do to the college in the community? We don't know the community well enough to know how provincial it is or how much race prejudice there may be. Should these kids get married it might mean the complete rejection of the college by the community."

Yet there was no question of what the college's position should be. The only question was whether those of us responsible for the college were strong enough to live up to our commitment.

Of course, I was concerned about the young couple and was hopeful that the prediction of the marriage by the father was the product of over-anxiety on his part. I had serious doubts in respect to the success of any such marriage. I had often pointed out the difficulties of a Negro-white marriage in a prejudice-ridden society in my lectures after having laid down the general thesis of individual rights and freedom of choice. Soon I had a chance to express these same doubts to the young couple, for within a few days Mr. Rushmore, much more composed and much calmer, asked me if I would see them.

So it was that I found myself facing the two young people seated together on the sofa in our living room. Doug was a handsome Negro boy of medium height. He impressed me as being intelligent and determined. Barbara Rushmore was a slender girl with brown hair. She appeared concerned, nervous and had a hint of defiance about her.

Doug came directly to the point: "Dr. Ritchie, will we be allowed to come back to school if we continue to keep company?"

"You are duly enrolled, aren't you? Both of you have passing grades, haven't you?"

"Yes, indeed."

"It seems to me, then, you have as much right to be at Hartwick as any other students."

The young couple sat quietly, just looking at me as if waiting for the catch, the qualifying statement that would contradict what I just said. When it did not come, Doug burst out. "But if we get married?"

"So far as I know," I said, "Hartwick College makes no distinction between married and unmarried students."

Obviously relieved, they asked if they might rent an apartment in the students' housing after their marriage. "If a vacancy exists, yes," I said. "The business manager has charge of these matters."

The couple sat quietly as if slightly stunned, and I felt that perhaps I should clarify further my attitude.

"Please understand," I said, "that as president of the college I am not approving or disapproving the idea of your marriage. An institution, in my view, does not have the right to interfere with free choice in such a matter. On the other hand, it is my view that a Negro-white marriage in our present society has many odds against it."

Perhaps encouraged by my frankness and also my insistence upon institutional non-interference, Barbara and Doug told me their story.

The girl's father, as I have already stated, was a successful attorney in a small upstate New York town. Barbara's parents, according to her report, had been over-protective. Dates were frowned upon but casual acquaintances encouraged. After college enrollment her close parental supervision continued, sorority membership was discouraged and trips home on weekends encouraged. The consequence was very little social involvement on the campus.

The boy's background was interesting. His mother was a mixture of Indian, white and Negro. His father was Negro with an eighth grade education. The mother had gone as far as the tenth grade.

Doug's early years with his parents were scarred by poverty. Later, after his parents divorced, he lived with his grandmother and things were better. The neighborhood was largely white and, with support from his parents, the household was maintained at about the same standard as those of the white neighbors.

Although Doug did well in high school, he had no plans for college. However, his athletic record in high school, together with his singing voice, earned him a tuition scholarship at Hartwick. Barbara was not the first white girl he had dated. There had been others in high school, but the dates had not included high school functions.

Some of the social forces which had drawn Doug and Barbara together were obvious from the description. She was a sensitive girl, and she had found in Doug a way to rebel against what she considered over-protection and also social prejudice. Incidentally, he reported that his own people did not approve of the prospective marriage. Some of his relatives predicted "trouble" and made it perfectly clear that they feared he would be denied job opportunities not only because he was Negro, but because he would break the Negro-white taboo.

"You must realize," I said to the young couple, "the serious problems you would face. Your marriage would limit the areas in which you might be able to live and the jobs you might be able to get. In some states your marriage would not be legal.*

"Of course, your marriage will not be breaking any law of God, for every human being is precious in His sight. But just the same, you would be violating perhaps the strongest social taboo for a majority of people in this country. I am a native of the South where this taboo is particularly strong, but I can assure you that the taboo also exists in the minds of many people who live in areas outside of the South.

"If you do marry, you should consider making your life in a large city where there is more sophistication about these matters. Of course, you can try to be heroes in the small community, but heroes are often extremely lonely people. Your love would have to be almost superhuman in order to live through the disappointments and humiliations that most likely would come your way."

Barbara and Doug were sober-looking when they left, and I was convinced that I had set them to thinking deeply but I had a feeling that nothing I said had changed their minds.

I heartily wished for the moment that I was back in the South where the law would have protected me from such problems. Of course I knew that the law through the decades had not prevented interracial mixing, just interracial marriage. Here in upstate New York was a Negro-white marriage in the making. And I found myself almost as concerned as the parents, but for different reasons. For one thing I feared the possibility of shrill treatment of the situation by the newspapers. However correct a nonintervention policy on the part of the college might be, any critics in the community would interpret such as full-fledged approval of the marriage. It seemed to me the greatest danger lay in giving special attention to the situation. Such special attention could be the basis of a devastating newspaper report.

The next day after my interview with Doug and Barbara at our house, I again called the Hartwick College deans into my office. Very plainly I reminded them of the non-discriminatory policy of the college in respect to race. I instructed them to avoid

---

* A recent United States Supreme Court decision has struck down anti-miscegenation laws in the states.

any special notice of the couple, but to accord them the same privileges as anybody else. Of course, I knew that the deans realized the situation could be serious.

One day in the early fall Barbara and Doug came to see me and asked whether their wedding could be held in the college chapel. I said, "No." I gave two reasons. The chapel was still under construction and was not suitable. But more important, a quasi-public ceremony would mean that the maudlin and curious would be there, invited or not, and so would reporters from the more sensational newspapers in New York City. I suggested they have a quiet wedding ceremony with their real friends in attendance. They were married, without incident, about two months after the fall semester began at Hartwick. In December they moved into a university apartment.

Barbara's parents accepted the marriage with remarkable understanding. Afterwards I was a guest in the Rushmore home and felt a deep sense of admiration for the parents in their role in what at that time (1953) was a very difficult situation.

A routine account of the Jones wedding appeared in the *Oneonta Star*. I had cautioned them against publishing wedding pictures. Several weeks passed before the townspeople realized there had been a student interracial marriage. It was several weeks before fellow Rotarians questioned me about it. When they asked why we did not take contrary action, I always turned the question to them saying, "What would you do in a Christian college?"

Undoubtedly there was criticism in the community and we heard rumblings of it, but there were no threats and no moves on anybody's part to withdraw support from the college. Later individual members of the board of trustees asked me about the matter. I simply told them that I followed the principle of non-discrimination and the Christian tenets of the college as best I could. Never once did the Trustees call me on the carpet about the matter, although there was a bit of head shaking on the part of one or two in view of the negative reaction that might have occurred.

Douglas and Barbara Jones lived quietly in a campus apartment until both graduated. Then they moved away to face "the facts of life" in professional advancement and community acceptance. But that is another story.*

We were very fortunate at Hartwick that the marriage of Doug and Barbara Jones caused so little excitement. In another Northeastern college not too long after this incident the courtship of a Negro student with a white student not only caused difficulty on the campus, but burst forth in extremely negative publicity in the New York papers and undoubtedly caused many sleepless nights for the president and great concern for other members of the university community. Whether the young people ever married I do not know.

The experience at Hartwick and my acquaintance with other episodes of Negro-white courtship have convinced me that a quiet evaluation of the policy considerations involved and an equally quiet putting into practice of those policies is the best approach. Extensive discussion by a variety of groups in the university family, unless absolutely necessary, may cause dissension, as well as almost inevitable publicity. And the press, no matter how sincere and honest in reporting, will likely highlight the most easily observed aspect of the situation and may miss many of the important points that are beneath the surface.

In my more than sixteen years of the college presidency, this has been the only Negro-white marriage which has occurred on the two campuses I have served. Though there are relatively few studies on this matter, it is my feeling that the percentage of such occurrences nationally will continue to be relatively small. The extreme fear of general miscegenation that has been felt on the part of leaders opposing integration in the schools is unfounded, I believe. In fact, it just may be that the years ahead will bring less rather than more miscegenation. In our grandfather's day, in certain parts of the country, the two-family system—one white and one mixed with one father, was commonplace. Today the Negro, due to education and increasing opportunity, economic strength and recognition of his rights, has increased reason to take pride in his racial identity. Certainly it is true that the Negro is not interested in becoming a white citizen;

---

* Mr. and Mrs. Jones have been happily married for 16 years and still live in upstate New York.

he is rather interested in becoming a full-fledged citizen with every opportunity that any other citizen has. On the other hand, it may very well be that a by-product of the close association of students of different cultures and races on the American campus may bring about a numerical increase of student marriages across cultural and racial lines. I do not look for any "rash" of such marriages.

As to policy, what should colleges do? Ignore such courtship and prospective marriages? Assume that no special problems are involved in such possible marriages? Certainly in the case of Doug and Barbara Jones, special problems were involved. In other cases with which I am acquainted, even without the prospect of marriage, problems sometimes do arise in which racial difference is presumably the causal factor. It seems to me that college administrations have the responsibility of thinking about these problems and of seeking to minimize the problems as much as possible in order to insure a normal social experience to every extent possible for their students. Certainly a college ought not to be two-faced in respect to interracial student courtship and marriage. It cannot honestly admit students of all races and then deny any group rights or privileges accorded to other groups. Despite what I've said about the probably continuing statistical insignificance of Negro-white marriages, when a Negro and white student begin to go together on a campus these statistics aren't very significant. All too often everybody assumes that the romance is certain to lead to matrimony and that the marriage will be faced with all sorts of earthshaking negative consequences.

One such case occurred at Pacific University some years ago. A white girl from the Northwest started keeping company with a young Negro student from Africa. Both were nice, sincere young people. I learned of it when the hometown minister contacted the University. The girl's parents, greatly agitated, came to campus. I tried to let the dean of students and the chaplain handle the matter, but finally the father came to me.

Again the story of Hartwick was repeated in the conversation. In effect he said: "You must stop their going together. I did not send my daughter to college to get involved in such a relationship." My response: "The University is willing to counsel the couple just as it would any other couple with widely different backgrounds."

But, I pointed out: "The University which tries to practice, to the limits of its capacity, both democratic and Christian principles cannot set up discriminatory bars."

Somewhere along the line I said: "The girl can always say 'No.'"

Again in the conversation I learned the young lady, coming from a small community, had limited experience with minority group persons. She had fine ideals and seemed to feel that this was her special way of proving her acceptance of the other person.

We counseled the parents to take "the pressure" off and to contain their extreme fears so that the case would not become "celebrated" on campus. Officially we gave it no recognition.

In a few months the young couple had other interests and we heard nothing more about the case. Had we followed an arbitrary, prescriptive line, I believe the situation might possibly have developed to the point of marriage and serious difficulties might have been encountered. These difficulties would not have been entirely racial in the origin, but certainly would have involved the wide difference in cultural background of the young people, the girl from the very rural Northwest, the boy from a vastly different African environment.

On most campuses and in communities of my acquaintance the attitude toward courtship and marriage between Mongoloids and Caucasoids is much less negative than in the case of Negroid-Caucasoid association. One father from Hawaii of Oriental extraction was reported to me as saying that he felt the probabilities to be very strong that his daughter would marry a Caucasian, since she was being educated on the mainland and would have opportunity to study and work together with students of this race. The young lady dated white boys while at Pacific, but did not marry while in college.

A lady of Chinese extraction, in commenting on the same probability in her daughter's case, expressed the hope that the University might have a number of "fine Chinese boys on the campus." Although understanding the developments of modern

91

times, she was negative in respect to her daughter marrying other than in her own cultural and racial group. The common opinion held by many that people of a minority racial group generally would like their children to marry into a majority group is certainly not necessarily true. I know of many cases in which the parents of the minority group person were unhappy and apprehensive in regard to the prospective marriage with a person from the majority group.

Assuming that the integrated character of campuses may stimulate some increase in the number of black-white marriages, what can college communities do about attitudes? I think the same rule applies here as in other changes in race relations.

People marveled that Louisville, Kentucky, desegregated its schools in 1956 with so little turmoil. The reason: Louisville was prepared. The documented story is told in *The Louisville Story,* an excellent book by Omer Carmichael, then superintendent of schools.

In Miami, Florida, the same surprise was expressed when the public schools and the private University of Miami admitted Negroes with so little fuss. At least the partial reason: long public discussion and education in intergroup relations.

Before 1953 while I was chairman of the Department of Human Relations at the University of Miami, much of this was going on. The University cooperated with the public schools, the Anti-defamation League, the National Conference of Christians and Jews, and other organizations to form the Dade County Intergroup Education Committee that brought Negro and white teachers together to discuss mutual problems.

The Department of Human Relations conducted short courses in intergroup relations for police department and other supervisory departments of Miami city government. A teachers' institute in intergroup relations was held on the University campus twice during my three-year chairmanship of the Department. Negro teachers in large numbers attended the non-segregated sessions, including luncheons and dinners.

Before I left Miami to go to the Hartwick presidency in 1953, hard and fast segregation was voluntarily broken. There were non-segregated conventions, auditorium meetings, periodic dinners, television appearances, church experiences, and many other non-segregated occasions. Though the situation nearly a decade later, when general desegregation in the schools and the colleges took place, was far from perfect, it was sophisticated enough for orderly change to take place.

Every university should help its community to understand the facts about racial, religious, national background, and ethnic differences. If the university has a good faculty and relates well to its community, it has the resources for such leadership.

The current development of black studies courses is in general a good thing. It will help fill a serious cultural vacuum. Such courses should have full academic credit and should be a part of the regular curriculum with the very best instruction available. Black studies will be helpful to Negro students not only intellectually but emotionally, and in some respects such courses will be even more helpful to students of other races.

Every community today cannot escape the responsibility to be world-minded, even if it is interested only in regional or national advantages. To be world-minded means understanding people of many shades and colors, eyebrow slants, eating habits, and cultural differences. A community which has such understanding may not approve, but will certainly not blow apart in the relatively rare situations which involve marriages across Negro-white lines.

If large-scale interplanetary travel does become a reality as predicted by some scientists and should human-like creatures be found on any planet—perhaps beautiful girls with dainty horns as in the "Dick Tracy" comic—we may have an "Earthling-Martian Taboo" and the differences between earthlings may seem much less important than they do now!

In the meantime, every college community must handle present problems with all possible intelligence and understanding.

CHAPTER VI

The Wilderness of Small College Finance

There was a day when small college finance was relatively simple. Some small colleges had wealthy individual "angels" who established and endowed them. Others even had groups of wealthy "angels" who did the same thing. Still others may not have had the good fortune to develop so much wealthy support from so few, but enjoyed vigorous support by their churches. A few fortunate institutions were able to combine church support with heavy support from wealthy individual donors.

Most of the college presidents fifty years ago were ministers. Either they or their representatives or both worked the church constituency very vigorously. Many a minister in those days would shudder when he heard that the church college prexy was headed his way. He knew that the philanthropic fatted calf would be picked down to the bare bones. Today the situation is radically different. The concept of the college as a missionary arm of the church has become less and less emphasized, and the college more and more has been accorded the role of a free institution dedicated to the search for truth rather than the dispensation of preconceptions masquerading as truth. And of course the educational process itself has become infinitely more complicated than it was in former days.

Great municipal and state universities have grown up while small, predominantly church-related colleges have increased in size and have been forced to become quality institutions or die. No longer is it sufficient for the local minister to exhort the church members to send their children to the denominational college simply because it is denominational.

The cost of providing an education has multiplied many times over, and the availability of increased numbers of students has brought both blessings and problems in respect to financing. The demand for admission has given the small private colleges courage to hike their tuition fees, but this demand also has made it necessary to provide additional buildings, equipment and faculty. Hence there is a pressing need in almost every small college in the country for both capital and operational funds. The tuition from the increased numbers of students has not kept pace with the increased salaries of faculty and the enormously increased cost of constructing new buildings and equipping them.

It is well known that many of the major universities have a very large part of their program financed by research grants from many sources, especially the federal government. Since most small colleges are not research oriented, they have been the step-children of such programs. In general, research programs have tended to make the big universities bigger and presumably the better ones more so, rather than helped to increase the quality of many smaller colleges which have been at a middle quality level and now are threatened with the fate of becoming mediocre or inferior, and in some cases with fading out of the picture altogether.

Smaller colleges generally have become larger. The college of 500 students in the mid-1940's now enrolls a thousand or more. Yet in many parts of the country there are colleges of less than 500 struggling to make a go of it. Of the nine accredited private senior colleges in Oregon in 1969, two of them enrolled less than 500 students.

The very tradition of the smaller college has caused serious financial problems. It proclaims itself as dedicated to the individual. The notion of small classes has been its stock in trade. All too often, however, professors in a small college insist upon defining small as meaning anywhere from five to ten students. With senior professors' salaries now in the better small colleges ranging from $12,000 to $20,000, classes of this size mean economic suicide unless the institution is the possessor of a magnificent endowment. Many small colleges have the tradition so strongly attached that it is almost impossible to break away from it and establish class patterns that are more sensible economically and still relatively speaking are small.

Even for the very able ministerial prexy who successfully led the financial campaign for his college among the supporting churches forty years ago, the situation today would be frustrating, frightening and most likely defeating. Today the small college president finds himself in a wilderness of finance with capital financial burdens on one shoulder and current operational burdens on the other and unclassifiable financial demands staring him in the face. In this financial wilderness the search for sustenance for his institution is infinitely complicated. Possibilities of government aid must be exploited, the related church must be continued in support, the parents must be urged to donate in addition to paying high tuition, private foundations must be wooed, cooperative college solicitation programs must be participated in, state funds if any must be sought, the alumni must be urged on to give till it hurts, life income programs must be devised emphasizing tax advantages as well as philanthropic instincts, and as always the person of individual wealth and generous motives must be courted day in and day out.

The president who is unwilling to engage in the practical business of fund-raising should resign immediately upon waking up to the real situation. Of course, if he doesn't resign he will get fired. Almost as bad is the president who seeks to do the entire job himself. He either will die early, or cease to be president and become only a fund-raiser. The statesmanship he ought to furnish the institution will soon dry up, and he will cease to have anything to raise funds for. Ideally the president insists upon not being a fund-raiser, but readily and effectively engages in raising funds. There is a difference. He should have a fund-raising officer and should develop a staff consistent with the size of the institution and, in addition, the largest possible aggregation of volunteers.

Of course, in many of the famous small colleges the boards of trustees consist of wealthy individuals who can set the pace. In some such colleges for more than a hundred years the graduates have been the sons of wealthy families and have thus provided a built-in giving constituency. But in many colleges this is not the case. The trustees have historically been ministers or alumni who are happy to help make policy decisions and to help run the institution, but either don't have the money to give or wouldn't give it if they had it. In such colleges the president and his fund-raising organization must either change the character of the board of trustees or develop volunteer donors and donation getters outside of the board. And if the alumni are all teachers and ministers, then they must be converted into ambassadors to the sources of wealth in their respective communities.

It is strange but true that a financial crisis is sometimes a real advantage. Such a situation demands action and often is so convincing that the action is forthcoming. If the crisis is successfully met under the leadership of the president, regardless of how many trustee advisors and co-workers he may have, his leadership is established and his support by the faculty and other elements of the constituency will be relatively unquestioned for a long time to come. It was precisely such a situation that I faced as the new president of Hartwick College in 1953. As has been mentioned in a foregoing chapter, I came to the presidency from a professorship and had little knowledge of the financial aspects of an institution. I had no experience in reading annual reports whether they were furnished by the college or the auditor. Institutional deficits had only a vague meaning. I did understand what being "broke" meant, since as a struggling young professor I had experienced this highly educative condition on numerous occasions.

But when I discovered that the desk of the business manager, who was also new at his job, was literally stuffed with unpaid bills reaching back a number of years I became concerned. Likewise when the representative of a local office supply house would not give me a regular 10% discount on a dictating machine "because the college didn't pay its bills" my curiosity about financial conditions was aroused.

At the first meeting of the executive and finance committees of the board of trustees someone knocked on the door and asked to see the president and no one else. I went to the door and greeted a chap in workman's clothes who said that he had a truckload of fuel oil but refused to unload it unless payment of the bill in cash was authorized, because the college was already heavily in debt to the company. Of course, I authorized cash payment of the bill, but the experience gave me quite a jolt and I returned to the meeting very sober indeed. The committees had lunch together and the business manager, Norm Roper, knowing that the day, July 24, 1953, was my 44th birthday, surprised me with a cake which the college chef had baked. The distinguished trustees tried to lift my spirits by singing "Happy Birthday" with great enthusiasm, but one board member put the whole thing in a nutshell when he said, "He's been with us a week and he's aged a year." So far as I was concerned it was the understatement of the week.

As I remember it, it was at this meeting or shortly thereafter that we arranged for Coville Winsor, a new member of the board who was also an expert on investments, to make a study of the financial condition of the college so that we would know where we were, however unpleasant the information might be.

By the fall meeting of the board it was clear that the college faced a deficit for the academic year of approximately $64,000 in a budget of less than $300,000. The total indebtedness of the college had now come to a point of some $135,000 and the total endowment of the college was only about $264,000.

Some concern had been expressed as to whether the college would receive money sufficient to complete the chapel wing of what is now Arnold Hall. Not being able to get any very clear information on the subject, I visited the headquarters of the United Lutheran Church in New York City and learned to my dismay that money sufficient to complete payment of the chapel would not be forthcoming and that the college faced the need for raising from some source well over $50,000 more than had been anticipated. The building was already under construction so there were no ifs, ands, or buts about it.

Adding to the capital situation was the fact that a women's dormitory, the generous gift of the Dewar Foundation, would have to be furnished and the kitchen and dining room equipped. This would be an additional substantial capital need.

Coville Winsor did a thorough job of analyzing the college's financial situation. It was a job that I could not possibly have done. I will always be grateful to this able trustee for reducing the complicated situation to simple figures that I could understand. When his final report came in it contained this statement: "From the auditor's report and from other financial records kept by the college, I am convinced that Hartwick College has been close to insolvency for some time." In dollars and cents the report made it very clear that the college desperately needed approximately $200,000 to put it in any kind of respectable shape.

Crises sometimes call for dramatic action. As a former professor, I astonished myself by the action I took. I told the board in effect that I did not intend to be the president of a dying institution and that the institution was going to rise from its sickbed and walk again. I said that it was obvious we had to raise money and in my opinion charity begins at home. I said that I was as poor as any man in the room, even the ministers, but that I would give in cash or in kind $1,000 to the college and I wanted to know what the members of the board were going to do.

I shall never forget Dr. Morris Skinner, a minister and chairman of the board. Although he had recently pledged $1,000 to the building effort in his own church, he said that he would "give or raise $1,000" and then he proceeded to poll every member of the board in attendance. In about thirty minutes over $12,000 was subscribed. Although this amount did not solve our problem, it was in some respects the most important step. From that moment on the Trustees were involved and committed to the fight to dig the college out of its financial troubles and to build it into a strong and healthy institution.

With the help of the trustees, staff, and community volunteers we took measures that only a crisis would have made possible. We got the local banks to agree that they would lend the college $110,000 to take care of its immediate needs on a mortgage basis, provided the church would increase our annual support by $7,000 to provide payments to retire the mortgage. Shortly thereafter I went before the supporting church in convention-assembled and urgently requested additional annual support, giving assurance that the banks had promised to come through with the loan. This was one time I played both ends against the middle for a good cause and won!

Although the college had only approximately 300 students enrolled, we jacked the tuition up $50 per year per student, gambling that Gerald E. Reese, the young admissions director we brought from Florida, would be able to get the students. He did, increasing the student body despite the increased cost about twenty-five percent that year.

We slashed athletic scholarships and scholarships in general. We refused a raise in salaries which was urgently needed but thoroughly impractical. I told the faculty frankly I didn't blame anybody who might wish to leave but hoped they would stay. They did. That is, except the part-time people whom I dropped with one or two exceptions.

Instead of increasing the number of faculty the next year with the increased number of students, we held firm; in fact, we reduced our faculty and staff to some extent. I assisted some of the younger people in getting better jobs elsewhere so the faculty would be brought more into line with the number of students. Unfortunately, my predecessor had not been able to bring himself to reduce the faculty in proportion to the reduction of students after the World War II veteran enrollment bulge had passed.

We called together the businessmen of the city and frankly laid before them the problems of Hartwick College, making it perfectly clear that the college was in deep trouble. The result was reassuring. The very men who had criticized the college for its financial problems suddenly realized that one of their major economic assets might disappear. They rolled up their sleeves and went to work with us. They established the Hartwick College Citizens Board which still operates to support the institution. Each year since its founding the members have raised a substantial sum of money in Oneonta for the support of Hartwick.

We went after small friendly foundations and individuals. We developed an alumni program and hired a full-time alumni secretary and publicity director. The Dewar Foundation gave us money to equip the new kitchen and the new commons on the first floor of the new dormitory. The Clark Foundation gave us money to support the School of Nursing. We went after small gifts of several hundred dollars each from people all over upstate New York for furnishing the rooms in the new dormitory. Economies were effected in every possible way, sometimes by simply saying "no." This applied to salary raises as well as to other things.

It was difficult for me, fresh from a professorship, to use the negative. I recall the case of one professor who demanded an increase in salary on the grounds that my predecessor had promised it. I reviewed the correspondence and found nothing that warranted such a claim in my opinion. The professor then threatened to sue the college. I told him to go ahead and sue, but he did not and continued on the faculty.

As has been mentioned, the college gained support from small family foundations in upstate New York, and from the alumni and the community. But the principal means of substantial assistance during the six years of my presidency came from individuals. An analysis of the sources of wealth in the area served by the college revealed that in the upstate New York area there resided a substantial number of wealthy individuals. Every effort was made to reach as many as possible.

The operating gifts to the college in 1958-59, our last year, showed a gain of 72% over the operating gifts in 1953-54, our first year. The budget had increased 118%. Capital gifts totalled $7,343.63 in 1953-54, and in our last year the total was approximately $1,2889,433. Although the Marion Yager bequest occurred during my last year, it was only partially recorded in the 1958-59 annual report, more than a half-million dollars of the bequest of approximately two million coming after the summer of 1959. The endowment, which was $263,339.72 in 1953-54, jumped to well in excess of $2,000,000 with the addition of the Yager Estate and other gifts and bequests.

When we left Hartwick for the West, many of our friends gave us a great deal of credit. And we were quite willing to accept our full share, for we had worked very, very hard. But during our time the college had been extremely fortunate in securing the cooperation of a substantial number of people, and in being the recipient of a number of bequests which might well have occurred five to ten years later.

101

Every person who interprets a college in respect to fund-raising should realize that the results of his efforts may not come in his time. Likewise, he must realize that often the gifts and bequests that do come in his time may have been initially stimulated by someone who lived years before. Each person who labors in the collegiate vineyard must plant and cultivate with all the wisdom he can, but he must not expect to see all the fruitage during his tenure.

During our administration at Hartwick we faced not only the need for new buildings, but the lamentably dilapidated condition of old buildings. To save money and get the job done we even organized student-faculty volunteer squads and painted the first floor interior of the administration building. Every building on the campus was in need of repair and renovation. We followed the practice of budgeting small funds for renovation each year. This practice continued until we had been there more than six years. In fact, as I recall it, it was during the summer of our last year that the old gymnasium got its fresh coat of barn-red paint.

Considerable new construction either was completed or initiated in our time. In 1954 the chapel wing of the Religion and Arts building was completed. In 1954 the first wing of Dewar Hall for women was dedicated. As has been mentioned, the Dewar Foundation made a second grant to insure the completion of this building and the equipping of the commons in the first floor of the building. In 1958 Leitzell Hall for men was dedicated. In 1959 a new wing for Dewar Hall was built including space for doubling the commons capacity and the providing of an excellent snack bar in the basement area.

Despite the building program, consistent efforts made it possible to reduce the mortgage debt and wipe it out. My final report entitled "Six Exciting Years" indicates that the trustees took action to this end before June of 1959.

My successor, Frederick M. Binder, continued to provide the leadership along with the trustees to place Hartwick College on an even firmer financial footing and at the same time to find foundation monies of a varied and substantial nature. Many sources of wealth that I didn't even know of were tapped. Many new buildings were built and the student body more than

102

doubled during Fred's nine years at Hartwick. I have watched this progress with great appreciation. And I am sure the spirits of Dr. Henry Arnold and Dr. Charles W. Leitzell must draw a similar satisfaction as they take their heavenly view of developments on Oyaron Hill.

A much more difficult financial situation to face is one of lethargy and defeatism. And this was the situation at Pacific University in 1959-60, despite the energetic work of my two predecessors, Dr. Walter Giersbach who had been president for some 12 years, and Dr. Charles Armstrong who had been president for about 5 years. Dr. Giersbach became the secretary for wills and bequests of the Stewardship Council of the United Church of Christ, and Dr. Armstrong became the president of the University of Nevada.

The peculiar situation at the University can be illustrated very well by a statement made to me by a leading businessman in the metropolitan Portland area. A few months after coming to Pacific University I approached him for a substantial contribution through his company's foundation. In the course of the conversation I asked him frankly why his company which has interests in Washington County had not contributed anything other than equipment to the one university in the same area. He said in effect the following: "No one from the University has really approached us. And frankly, our idea of the University is that it is a very shabby but respectable and ancient institution which isn't really too concerned about making much progress."

Perhaps his remarks were a bit strong, but in some respects they reflected the situation. The University had operated without a president for a year. Part of that time an administrative committee had provided leadership and then an acting president in the person of a retired Superintendent of the Oregon Congregational Conference, Dr. Paul Davies, handled administrative matters.

Although my two immediate predecessors had in many ways been strong presidents and although they had cultivated sources of money, there were many highly negative factors in the financial situation. Before I explore this point, however, let me say that sources of individual wealth cultivated by both Dr. Giersbach

103

and Dr. Armstrong have been very productive for the University either during their administration or since. Notable among these are the Judith Scott Walter Trust in California and the Washburne Trust in Eugene, Oregon, both established in favor of the University.

The negative factors were most apparent. The University was scarcely known in the metropolitan area of Portland. And when you asked anyone on campus whether the University got along well with its community, the reply was immediate: "Yes, indeed, Forest Grove and the University are more compatible, never any serious trouble." And sometimes in the very reply it was perfectly obvious that the college was taken for granted by the community and also that the college all too often took the community for granted.

But the thought that Pacific University's community really is the greater Portland metropolitan area seemed never to have entered anyone's head. Certainly it was obvious that no broad constituency had been developed in the greater Portland area. Practically no one at the University was active in the Portland area in a civic capacity, and the number of people on whom there was real data indicating continuing friendship for the college was very small.

There was no accurate, extensive alumni list, although the Assistant to the President, James N. Phinney, was vigorously working on the project at the time I arrived. And certainly the list he developed has been basic to the excellent alumni record at Pacific University during the decade since I arrived. Alumni came to the University from time to time for big dinners with extensive entertainment, but no habit of financial giving that amounted to anything had been developed.

There was practically no support from foundations and the contacts made with potential foundation supporters had been minor. Very small contributions of a special nature had been secured from the Congregational Church. Some monies came in from individual churches, but no substantial sum had been received for many years from the Congregational Church Boards.

Of course, in 1959 government grants to private colleges were not extensive, but Pacific had made little effort in this direction and had certainly received no support that amounted to anything. The only substantial government assistance had come in the form of a building loan for the construction of the first unit of Judith Scott Walter Hall.

The University had a history of deficits extending back for more than a decade with only two balanced budgets in the dozen years prior to 1959. The summer school was a tiny makeshift affair. The number of classes in both the summer and winter sessions with less than five students was astonishingly large.

Yet, there was no great crisis other than the constant complaints of creditors, the justified beefs of the faculty relative to poor pay, and the complaints of students, alumni, and visitors respecting the decrepit appearance of most of the buildings. There were no ugly incidents such as the Hartwick College oil supplier's demanding cash for his load of oil or the matter of the Oneonta salesman refusing a 10% discount on a dictating machine or the lady telling the new Hartwick president's wife that she had thrown the inaugural invitation into the wastebasket. There was openhanded hospitality and many apologies for the University's "problems," but there was always the notion implied or spoken that "old Pacific University has always been here and always will be."

Pacific's institutional illness was chronic, not acute. In some ways this situation was much more difficult to face than the one at Hartwick. My experience of over a half-dozen years in the presidency had alerted me to problem symptoms, and I knew that Pacific needed some remedial action. However, this same experience had made me more cautious and conservative in the approach.

I felt that the trusteees and the faculty must be involved, if for no other reason than to convince them that action needed to be taken on a fairly broad front. Accordingly, I suggested to the Trustees a long-range planning study by a committee representing Trustees, faculty and administration. This committee was chaired by Trustee Robert Hansberger, president of Boise Cascade Corporation.

The committee brought out its report in the winter of 1960-61.

105

It was adopted by the faculty and the trustees and called the Program of the Sixties for want of a better name.

The committee did not seek to develop any dramatic, novel objectives; rather it stressed the need for a sense of balance in education and really committed the University to improvement of what was there rather than sweeping it aside for something new. The committee's report said that "Pacific University's general purpose is to provide a collegiate experience out of which the best balanced leadership can develop." Then it outlined twelve specific objectives, as follows:

1. To see the total impact of Pacific University in the light of its motto: Pro Christo et Regno Ejus (For Christ and His Kingdom).

2. To maintain a faculty of superior competence in professional functions and of exemplary quality in personal life.

3. To foster continuous professional growth among the faculty and to provide the working conditions that best promote creative teaching and relevant scholarly pursuits.

4. To maintain a program of studies that relates the traditions of our heritage to problems of contemporary life.

5. To encourage every student in his search for ultimate truth by offering courses that deal with the fundamental issues of life, and by showing genuine concern for his worth as an individual.

6. To involve students in a social experience in and out of the classroom, which will prepare them for successful participation and leadership in American and world society.

7. To maintain a core of liberal arts as "the heart" of the academic program of the University and to relate it effectively to the professional studies and career planning of the individual student.

8. To preserve the "sense of community" that the smaller college can provide, with its special sensitity to human values both individual and group.

9. To encourage in every student an appreciation of the individual's contribution to society and to stimulate him to recognize and discharge his responsibilities and to accept his unique role in the pioneering opportunities of our age.

10. To continue an interest in the career and personal welfare of each student after he has left the campus.
11. To serve as a cultural center for all the publics of the University.
12. To maintain and develop the historic campus in Forest Grove so as to provide optimum educational facilities and equipment.

Among other things the report stressed that the University needed to examine its academic offerings, analyze its organizational structure, study carefully its operational approach, improve its salaries, seek added endowment, and build a substantial number of new buildings and renovate the old ones. The limit of the undergraduate student body was set at 1200.

Projected new buildings or additions to existing buildings included the following units: Two additions to Judith Scott Walter Hall (women's residence hall), a university center, a large addition to the library, a third floor to the College of Optometry, a new gymnasium, a music center, and a science center. Securing $4,000,000 in additional endowment was cited as an important need and the total bill for all these improvements was figured to be $10,000,000.

The plan was announced in March 1961, although actual fund-raising did not get under way to any great extent until 1962. One of our graduates recently wrote me respecting the announcement as follows:

"When we were freshmen in the Fall of 1960, many students and, perhaps more secretly, many faculty members, regarded this ambitious plan skeptically as far too unrealistic to ever find realization. But we are learning how determined, dedicated effort can bring about such a worthy cause."

His comments only verified reports I had from people in the community and my own suspicions.

By September of 1969, however, we had more than accomplished the ten-million-dollar objective. Total funds secured, including low-cost government loans as of September 1, 1969, stood at approximately $11,000,000.

Funds have been secured from a number of sources, including foundations, the supporting church, alumni, parents, and private

107

individuals. In more recent years substantial monies have been secured from the federal government both in the form of grants and low-cost loans. And in 1969 Pacific along with other private universities began to benefit from a state financial aid program. Some of the sources of funds were relatively untapped at the beginning of the decade.

The building goals as outlined in the Program of the Sixties have been approximately reached but have taken many forms not provided for in the planning. As in the case of most such long-range plans, new ideas and improvements occurred as the effort continued.

In 1964 a new million-dollar university center was dedicated with the principal address being delivered by the then governor, Mark O. Hatfield. The university center includes dining facilities along with space for a large bookstore and a modern infirmary. The space vacated by the infirmary and the commons in old McCormick Hall was then converted into dormitory rooms. The old, inadequate student union building was immediately converted into a building for the art department.

Only one new wing was built to Judith Scott Walter Hall in 1962. Instead of the second wing a new building, Harvey Clarke Hall, was built to house 200 students. Dedication was held October 16, 1966.

Instead of a new third floor in the College of Optometry building, an addition was built incorporating the old building as one small wing, the total cost being some four times what was originally planned. The building was dedicated June 30, 1967.

The Program of the Sixties envisioned an addition to the Carnegie library building, but this idea was discarded and an entirely new building was constructed and named for Harvey W. Scott, first graduate of the University. The new building dwarfed the originally planned addition to the old library, and has space for 240,000 books. The library was dedicated on November 11, 1967. At this writing the old library is being converted into an air-conditioned classroom building.

Two more buildings were envisioned by the Program of the Sixties. This objective is being realized somewhat differently than originally planned and the development is much to the advantage of the University.

In late 1968 the University purchased the Lincoln Junior High School property, and at this writing a new university gymnasium-fieldhouse is under construction. The building will be substantially larger than had been anticipated in early planning. As soon as the present junior high school building is vacated, it will be converted into a classroom building to serve the sciences and the music school. The music facility will consist of a new recital hall developed in the space now used for gymnasium purposes. Later an additional wing or a nearby separate building will be provided for practice rooms for the music school.

Fortunate bequests have added approximately two million dollars to the University's endowments and trusts. In this particular category the goal of $4,000,000 has not been reached.

The University is now getting extensive press coverage, the enrollment has risen to approximately 1200 students, and alumni pride in the University is evidenced not only in what they write, say and do but also in a healthy annual contribution through the alumni fund. Faculty salaries have risen approximately 100% during the decade, and the 1969 summer issue of the Association of University Professors journal rates Pacific very favorably for its sharp improvement in salaries.

These are very encouraging developments. How did they come about? Mostly by hard work on the part of a great many people. There was no magic. Of course the situation was analyzed by the president of the University and by various others.

The fund-raising involved complicated activities and experienced various delays and discouraging lulls. At the outset of the effort the supporting church gave $100,000 as "seed money." And this was an important impetus to the success of the program. Certain key individuals and foundations made fairly substantial gifts and these tended to stimulate others. Extremely important was the fine response of alumni and the Forest Grove community. One of the weakest points in the effort was the absence of any very large gifts. This made the fund-raising all the harder. But this disadvantage had a bright side in that the large number of people giving provided for Pacific University for the first time a broad base of financial support, both present and future. Fund-raising in the greater Portland area played a large part, along with press coverage and the civic activities of the president and others in developing a new and favorable image of Pacific University.

In the current major building project, including the new gymnasium-fieldhouse, the conversion of the Lincoln Junior High School building, and the conversion of the old library for other purposes, low-cost government loans have for the first time been used heavily in non-income producing construction. The reason for this is that the University had an unusual opportunity to secure the junior high school property and thus to wrap up its major building needs in one project. The other principal reason was the very obvious fact that government loan money available at 3% when the prime rate is 8½% almost amounts to a grant. The drawback, however, is that considerable additional fund-raising will need to be engaged in to retire the loan. But such a maneuver does bring into operation much more rapidly many needed new or converted facilities.

The University, like many other small institutions, has suffered from the double load of securing substantial capital gifts and supplementary operational funds simultaneously. The budget has more than tripled, going from less than a million in 1959 to $3,168,600 for 1969-70. Added strength in current financing has been developed through increased tuition charges and through current fund-raising efforts of various kinds, but the bugaboo of deficits has not been eliminated. Only two substantial surpluses have been recorded in the more than ten years that I have been at Pacific. Analysis of these problems continues and their importance is fully appreciated.

Pacific's financial problems are all too typical of those in many other smaller private institutions. In all of these institutions an earnest search for solutions is pressed day and night. Some institutions will not find the solutions. In the next twenty years many small colleges will be taken over by the state, will consolidate with other colleges, or will close their doors.

Those that survive and continue to grow and develop will have to make some hardheaded decisions as well as to perform unselfish services. One of these decisions will have to do with tuition and fees. Tuition and other costs will need to continue upward as a principal means of income. Private colleges will be forced to cater to families of middle or high incomes. Of course, to the extent possible they will provide scholarship monies to enable students of limited means to attend. But the admissions emphasis will inevitably point in the direction of the family of financial adequacy.

The aversion of some small colleges toward government assistance soon will virtually disappear. There is not too much of it left now. Church related colleges which fear court action preventing their qualifying for government funds will amend their church relatedness in such a way as to make themselves eligible. Where there are exceptions to this, the supporting churches will have to increase radically the level of their support in order to offset the loss of government funds. One reason that the church related college will seek to insure eligibility for government funds is that most churches have failed miserably in showing any adequate effort to support the colleges which they claim as their academic offspring. Major dependence upon church support would mean financial starvation in the vast majority of cases.

Smaller private colleges will need to stop complaining about the fact that foundations have largely overlooked them and will need to find means of convincing foundations that they have a unique contribution to make. Generally the leadership in smaller colleges has been inept and unimaginative in its approach to foundations for support. Certainly the executives and the trustees of foundations do not deserve all the blame for short-changing the smaller colleges and universities in distributing the vast funds at their disposal.

Though business support to small colleges has risen substantially in recent years, especially through the cooperative association approach, support of business must be increased if private higher education is to survive. Such an investment on the part of business is reasonable, since tax laws encourage it and since the private colleges in many respects represent the last stronghold of the private enterprise principle in the educational community. And further, business and industry draw some of the best talent for corporate leadership from the smaller private colleges. Again,

111

the onus is on the leadership of the smaller colleges and their trustees to see that the needs and potential of the small colleges are presented to business and industry in a convincing light.

My own experience with business and industrial leaders is that they are sympathetic to the ideals and objectives of small colleges, though sometimes skeptical as to the efficiency with which they operate. Businessmen today are well informed about higher education in general. They don't have to be convinced that the business community depends upon higher institutions of learning of various kinds for its future leadership, for consultant services, and for pioneering research. But the role which the small private college can play needs to be emphatically and imaginatively impressed upon business. The relative isolation of the smaller private college from the business community must be eliminated and interaction of the most positive kind must be developed to the greatest possible extent. Out of such a relationship could come the support which will insure survival and continued growth.

Smaller private colleges generally have been very slow in developing well-manned, efficient development programs. Some of these colleges have been too small to sustain a development office. Others have hesitated to pay substantial salaries to "money raisers," and have feared the criticism of faculty and other administrators who draw lower pay. This is a strange phenomenon, for the success of a development program will guarantee the higher salaries that other administrative officials and the faculty so vigorously demand.

The oft-repeated faculty comment that good teaching recommends itself and that gifts will come to the institution that is first rate without the activities of a development department simply is not true. The "better mousetrap" story does not apply to education, and there may be some doubt as to whether it ever applied to "mousetraps." Even the best college must have the personnel and procedures to find sources of financial support and to convince these sources that an investment in the institution is not only warranted, but desirable.

Part of a development program has to be long-range, especially with regard to life income contracts and bequests. Results cannot be expected overnight. Too few colleges are investing in personnel to exploit positively the opportunities for such support.

Beardsley Ruml and Donald Morrison in their book, *Memo to A College Trustee,* emphasize the importance of developing greater efficiency in colleges.[1] Essentially the book is sound. Perhaps it overlooks some of the enormous elements of tradition and other factors which stand in the way of a transformation of colleges. But it is perfectly true that many colleges, particularly smaller private colleges, operate or have operated in a highly inefficient manner. Even today, on many a campus, a person could shoot a rifle across the campus in the late afternoon without much danger of hitting anyone. He might strike one of the new buildings, but the likelihood of every room being occupied is very remote. Likewise, the same campus may be almost deserted at nighttime except for the dormitories and the student center. The classrooms are dark and empty.

Although year-round operation, whether on a trimester basis or with an active summer school, has become increasingly the practice among colleges, there are still many campuses with activities entirely closed during the summer months.

The number of courses offered in many of our smaller colleges is entirely out of keeping with the size of the student body. All too often these courses are added because they fit the interest of the professors rather than the needs of the students. The result is upper division classes of five to ten instead of twenty to twenty-five. Such practices will spell economic ruin for the smaller private college. And yet, making changes that appear relatively obvious is not easy. In my own case I have urged many of these changes at Pacific University, have directed that some of them take place and have personally been involved in the effectuating of others. The net result is that after ten years as president I can point to only a modest percentage of the changes that should take place as having been accomplished.

One of the changes that appears to be entirely practical is to develop cooperative groupings of colleges. This is taking place in various parts of the country. Colleges situated within 25 miles

---

[1] *Memo To a College Trustee* by Beardsley Ruml/Donald H. Morrison, McGraw-Hill Book Company, 1959.

of each other can very conveniently exchange professors, consolidate small classes, merge library resources, hire lecturers and artists at a saving, engage in common purchasing, and do a host of other things at great economy and profit to the institutions involved. Such cooperative association will most assuredly grow and become a well accepted pattern in private higher education.

In Oregon we have scarcely begun cooperative efforts, but the establishment of the Oregon Independent Colleges Association has been an important first step. Various cooperative activities have taken place such as conferences of the deans of all the private colleges, the business managers of all the private colleges, active cooperation by admissions directors, developing a common front on key tax issues before the legislature, and a number of other important developments. The financial aid voted to private colleges by the state legislature this year is a direct result of efforts by the Oregon Independent Colleges Association.

Some years ago I proposed in a public statement that library resources of nearby institutions be used cooperatively. Certainly not as a result of my statement but as a result of extensive planning and organization on the part of representatives of a new organization, The Northwest Association of Private Colleges and Universities, a federal grant of $225,000 has been received for mutual improvement of libraries in the area.

The very nature of smaller private colleges sometimes gets in the way of developing greater efficiency. They are wrapped in tradition. They tend to have faculties who may appear to be liberal in some ways, but mark themselves as rank conservatives when there is any question of change. Sometimes creation of greater efficiency involves the question of efficiency versus human value. Consequently inefficient persons are often sustained in jobs when perhaps changes might have promoted efficiency. All of this adds up to a relatively slow pace of change. Nonetheless, it appears that many leaders in the smaller private colleges have gained an awareness of the direction that must be taken, and are beginning to find their way through the wilderness of finance. Yet, the promised land is always a far distance.

CHAPTER VII

Prexy Goes After the Cash

About fifteen years ago, while on a fund-raising mission for the Empire State Foundation, I opened the door of the New York offices of a corporation president. My teammate in the fund-raising, Mother Helene, entered, wearing the habit of her order.

A comely receptionist nodded respectfully, reached in the desk drawer, took out a 50¢ piece and plopped it into the hand of the astonished nun.

Hastily she said to the young lady, "But, I am not a begging nun. I am the president of Nazareth College."

Indicating me, she added, "Along with President Ritchie, I am here to interview the head of your company."

Of course, the receptionist was almost overcome with embarrassment, as Mother Helene kindly returned the 50¢ piece. Much flustered, the young lady ushered us in to see the president of the company.

Later in the day the story was picked up by a New York Times reporter at a luncheon meeting of the presidents. In the Times I was quoted as having said to Mother Helene just after she returned the 50¢ piece to the young lady: "But, Mother, you shouldn't have given the money back. We need every cent."

In one gesture the receptionist in this business office had inadvertently classified a college president as a beggar. And in the minds of many people she was not far wrong. Undoubtedly the popular conception of a college president today is that of a generalissimo of fund-raising in higher education.

It is also true that most selection committees seeking presi-

115

dents for private colleges place fund-raising ability high on the list of qualifications. Yet I believe that most of them would applaud my previous statement that a college president should never allow himself to be just a fund-raiser. If he does, he will certainly cease to be an able president. At the same time, I am sure there would be very strong applause for my further statement that the president does need to be willing to be involved in fund-raising. There is a considerable difference. I'm afraid, however, that the average person interested in higher education and possibly the average member of a election committee do not stop to consider the difference.

In any case, the president of a college today must be involved in the fund-raising process, must have a concern for the strategy of fund-raising, and must be sophisticated respecting ways and means of developing these resources for his institution. Analyzing the constituency for financial resources is a major function of the president's office, together with his development staff, for the president must recommend to the trustees the crucial decisions concerning fund-raising efforts.

At Hartwick College in New York State in 1953 when I engaged in such an analysis, it was obvious that most of the money available was in the hands of individuals and small family or company foundations, since there was very little industry in any nearby area of the state. Hence, the primary emphasis upon immediate and long-range gifts and bequests from individuals and the vigorous cultivation of foundations in the direction of donations for special projects.

The greater Portland area contains a vast variety of business firms, and the percentage of individuals of wealth interested in supporting higher education is small in comparison with the situation in upstate New York. Hence, the Pacific University development program must be geared to industry as well as to individuals and foundations. Each prospective donor needs to be studied in terms of his likes and dislikes, his aspirations and his interests. Then the approach should be developed in terms of the kinds of challenge the individual is likely to respond to.

In any fund-raising effort by the institution, there will be those people who will respond only to the president before making

116

the final decision respecting a gift. It may be that they insist upon the prestige attached to being approached by the president, or it may be that they want the reassurance respecting the uses of their donation that only the president can give. Sometimes only the president can serve as the "ice breaker," initiating the relationship and letting the development staff follow up in bringing it to successful fruition.

In other cases the president comes into the picture quite late as an interpreter of institutional policy and of the institution's specific plans that may be relevant to the gift. In addition, the president often carries a small group of possible donors on a list for continuous cultivation. Many of these people may be current donors and excellent prospects for bequests.

Obviously, an enlightened board of trustees would not expect the president of the institution to operate on a door to door, hand to hand, begging basis. But on the other hand, the president who feels it beneath him to approach a key prospect and really "sell" him on the needs of the institution simply is not in tune with the practical situation which faces independent colleges today. He should leave the presidency and go back to teaching, even if it is a course in the theory of administration. Anything to remove him from the practicalities of the job itself!

One of the significant break-throughs of recent years in college fund-raising has been the enlistment of general participation by business firms in the ongoing support of private institutions of higher learning. Much of this has come about through the state associations.

In the episode described in the beginning of this chapter Mother Helene and I were representing the Empire State Foundation. At least in the early years of this organization composed of more than twenty colleges in the state of New York, visits were made by pairs of presidents. It was felt necessary to put the presidents' prestige on the line to open the doors of corresponding officials in business. It worked. Generally throughout the country the same pattern has been used.

In our Oregon Colleges Foundation, of which I am a past president, the chief executives of the colleges have been the principal solicitors, although in more recent years an increasing share

117

of the calling has been done by trustees and development officers. But in the early stages of the Foundation the presidents knocked on most of the office doors.

In the sixteen years of my two presidencies I have observed a most encouraging change in the business climate as regards support for colleges. In 1953 I would frequently be asked by businessmen: "Why in the —— should I support colleges? My company manufactures nuts and bolts!" We gave them the best answers we could, and they proved to be effective. One such person later became a strong supporter of the Empire State Foundation.

Nowadays, the visiting president almost never hears such a statement. The answer may be "no," but it is not based on any disregard for the importance of the smaller college. The businessmen, especially the younger ones, are remarkably well informed on the subject and believe quite as firmly as the president in the importance of higher education to the American economy and to the private enterprise system.

It was refreshing to come to Oregon in 1959 and discover that the major banks in Portland were among the founders of the Oregon Colleges Foundation. This was in substantial contrast to the situation in New York where the banks were just beginning such support when I left the state.

The necessity to enlist the general support of business has had many values in addition to sheer dollars. One of these has been better understanding between private college presidents and business leaders. Old suspicions have been allayed. Business leaders have become, in the eyes of college presidents, more progressive than the stereotype has held them to be. By the same token, college presidents have generally turned out to be more conservative than the stereotype of the educator has previously pictured them.

Stalking the dollars in the canyons of Wall Street or in the green hills of Oregon has been for me an interesting and exhilarating human experience. From it have come many friends, along with substantial money for the institutions I have represented. And in the bargain there has been a number of surprising and sometimes amusing episodes.

In New York State I recall visiting the president of a technical

118

firm making airplane parts. He was an engineer, and I had prepared a real case for the liberal arts college. But I really never got around to my speech, for he launched into an eloquent testimonial to the value of liberal education by citing his own deficiencies as a somewhat narrowly trained professional engineer. He described in colorful language the effort he had made to supplement his education in the humanities and social sciences so as to be able to cope with a job that demanded administrative skills and public interpretation. There was no need to convert him. So we asked him to serve as the businessman chairman of our effort in his area. He proved to be a very valuable ally. Though his firm was unable to give a large sum, he proved to be a most valuable missionary in bringing other firms into the fold.

One day I visited Melvin Eaton, then president of the Norwich Pharmacal Co. It was one of my early visits on behalf of Hartwick College. We talked upstate New York politics a while and exchanged views on the glories of New York State in general as compared to other sections of the country where I had lived. He sympathized with my problems as the new president of Hartwick College, and I told him that it was a job in which I knew I would take a great deal of aspirin for the perpetual headaches that I would suffer. And I solemnly promised always to ask for Norwich aspirin. I still do.

As the result of this and numerous other visits, the Norwich Pharmacal Co. began to contribute with substantial generosity to Hartwick College. Then, years after I left for the West, the company foundation was a major donor to the new science hall constructed under Fred Binder's administration.

And speaking of drug firms, I visited one in another part of New York State after being told that the principal officer was difficult to approach. On entering his office I saw behind his desk a large portrait of Stonewall Jackson. Throwing into gear my ancestral southern drawl, I remarked on how nice it was to see "Cousin Stonewall's" picture on the wall. That was about all I got to say, for the businessman turned out to be an amateur Civil War historian and the writer of an unpublished volume on the subject. He told me more about the battles in my native state of Virginia and the exploits of the famous Stonewall in my native Shenandoah

Valley than I had ever known before. Unfortunately, after the wonderful common ground had been developed, he politely but firmly refused to make a donation to the cause of private higher education. As I recall it, we never got a cent from him or his firm!

But sometimes surprises run in the other direction. On behalf of the Oregon Colleges Foundation I called on the president of a highly respected lumber firm. He was a graduate of one of the California universities and a man of mature years. Previously contributions through the Foundation had been small, and really expectations from the call were minor. I gave him the usual pitch about the value of private higher education to the state of Oregon and the extent to which it saved taxes for the people. I also deftly tucked in the statement that the private college epitomizes private enterprise in higher education.

Apparently he didn't pay too much attention to what I was saying, and presently interrupted me to say in effect, "You know, I think I am going to make a contribution to Pacific University this year. I saw a television program about Pacific and it impressed me." There I was, caught with the wrong professional hat on. Hastily I reminded him that I was president of Pacific University and I appreciated his interest in that institution, but that on this occasion I was wearing the hats of all eleven colleges in the Oregon Colleges Foundation and would especially appreciate a contribution to the Foundation, though I certainly hoped he would contribute to Pacific as well. Perhaps it was courtesy or perhaps it was an expanding interest in higher education. At any rate, he did make a contribution both to the Foundation and to Pacific University. And the contribution was larger than he had made in previous years. Naturally, I went away pleased as Punch with my faith in human generosity restored.

Sometimes crystalizing the interest of a company or individual takes more than one effort. At Pacific University our first approaches to Tektronix, the great Oregon electronic industry, bore no fruit. We emphasized a technical need, assuming it would attract interest, but it turned out not to be a technical need in line with the company's interests. Later we filed an application for assistance in hiring a new dean for one of our schools, but to

120

no avail. Then we invited the board of directors of the company foundation to visit the University, had a luncheon discussion concerning university needs, took a tour of the campus to demonstrate how we had used every available space, and then inspected the old library which we proposed to replace with a modern structure. After the visit we filed with the foundation a specific request for assistance on the new library project. The result eventually was a gift of $35,000.

Oftentimes gifts in kind are overlooked by both colleges and industrial firms. They are an excellent way of providing equipment for institutions of higher learning at minimum cost to the donor. In New York a branch of the Bendix Aviation Corporation made regular donations of equipment to the Physics Department of Hartwick College. At Pacific University, in 1966, the regional unit of the Varian Corporation donated an extremely useful electron microscope.

I have mentioned the chairman of the board at Hartwick, Dr. Morris Skinner. He was a source of great strength to us in many areas. His standing in the church and his ecumenical appreciation of the multi-religious backgrounds at Hartwick and the fact that resources must come from many different groups stood us in good stead when we were criticized by ultra-conservative elements in the supporting church. And his sturdy loyalty and complete faith in the mission of the college even under the most difficult circumstances served to inspire all the rest of us. He knew the difference between narrow denominationalism and broad Christianity and stood for the latter so far as the college was concerned. Other ministers on the board stood with him. Certainly financial support from the church more than doubled on an annual basis during my tenure, and capital gifts from the same source were largely a tribute to the leadership of the ministerial members of our board of trustees.

If a college is to raise money from its constituency, the board of trustees must set an example of generous investment in the institutional project, whatever it may be. If the trustees will not support it, then why should anybody else? Trustee gifts are the primer for a fund-raising effort.

I recall Clyde Bresee, who was chairman of the finance com-

121

mittee at Hartwick, in this connection. Clyde set an example by giving to the financial needs of Hartwick out of his own pocket. His standing in the community urged others to give. If he believed in the institution, others would believe in it. And in the rugged early days at Hartwick Clyde Bresee's example was a crucial factor in averting disaster and in laying the foundation for stability.

Among the laymen on the Hartwick board of my day I shall never forget Charles L. Ryder. He was a publisher of a string of weekly papers in upstate New York with headquarters at Cobleskill. When I first went to Hartwick I was warned that Charles would be hard to get along with, but I found him to be one of the most cooperative and deeply concerned trustees I have known. He was vice president of the board and chaired one of the important committees. I shall never forget the conferences we had together in laying the groundwork for committee consideration of key matters. One day Charles said to me in effect, "Mike, I'm not a rich man and I cannot give large sums, but I want very much to do my share. My income is good, and I would like to subscribe $100 a month from now on as long as I am able to pay it." So far as I know, the check came in regularly from then on until I left Hartwick. It undoubtedly has continued and perhaps much larger sums have come from this generous and dedicated man who has since become chairman of the board of trustees upon the untimely death of Dr. Skinner.

Someone had said that a trustee should be asked to make a commitment that he will either give or produce $10,000 a year for the institution on whose board he sits. Of course, I would not propose such a strict formula, but I do believe that asking a community leader, especially a well-to-do businessman, to come on the board of trustees calls for frankness and honesty. He should not be told that only his name, his wisdom and his prayers are wanted. He should also be told that his treasure is wanted. Sometimes this treasure does consist of skills that are the equivalent of money. Sometimes the good name of the trustee and his prominence in the community are valuable. But generally prestige will not discharge the obligations of a university budget. A trustee should give in cash or in kind or he should not be a trustee.

122

In our Program of the Sixties at Pacific University, John W. Pugh served as associate chairman of the Fund-raising Committee. At that time he was general secretary of the metropolitan YMCA in Portland and drew an adequate but modest salary. Yet he insisted on subscribing more to the library than I honestly thought he should in order to place himself in a psychological position honestly and enthusiastically to ask others to give. And his advice and leadership in actual solicitation were key factors in the successful financial effort to build a great new library at Pacific University.

On the subject of giving I have been extremely frank with the trustees both at Hartwick and at Pacific University. Our trustees at Pacific are giving substantially more than they did in the early days of my presidency. A few have resigned, some of them possibly because of the pressure in this regard. Sometimes trustees not only can be generous themselves, but can be instrumental simply by example in bringing the University to the attention of company foundations or company philanthropic committees.

Some years after I came to Pacific I went to see Reed O. Hunt, then president of the Crown Zellerbach Corporation. Mr. Hunt had served as a commencement speaker at Pacific University and Josephine and I had been entertained in his home. But on this occasion I went to his office in San Francisco and asked him to come on the board. It happened that another, much larger and more prestigious university was after him for the same purpose. I said to him quite earnestly, "Mr. Hunt, they don't need you as we do. There are many leaders in industry that would jump at the opportunity to go on that board of trustees. And besides, you would have more fun with us." Reed came on our board and has been an excellent trustee. He hasn't been able to attend meetings as often as some others, but he has been generous through his own private foundation and at least partially through his interest the needs of Pacific University have been brought to the attention of the company foundation. Of course, the approach has been directly to the officials of the foundation by the president of the University or other University representatives. In no case has Mr. Hunt been asked to twist arms.

Reed has been a most important adviser to the University and has hosted luncheons of key people in San Francisco as well as attending meetings in Forest Grove and Portland.

Not long after coming to Pacific, I heard of a man named Ray Replogle, vice president of the Stimson Lumber Co. I was told that he was not likely to be too interested in the University and would certainly not make any substantial contributions. Still, he was an important official of a nearby unit of one of the West's great business organizations.

Really my acquaintance with Ray was facilitated by my wife's becoming acquainted with Edith Replogle, his wife. She was interested in antiques and had a house full of them. Antiques are a keen interest of my wife. The common interest ripened into a warm friendship and through this friendship I learned to know Ray. He turned out to be one of the most warmhearted, and wonderful men I know.

In due time he introduced me to the head of the company Harold Miller. A friendly session with Mr. Miller ensued. I explained to him our needs, especially the need for a new library, but left without a commitment. I wondered whether we would get a donation at all and if so, how much. Then one day the telephone rang and Ray told me that the company had decided to contribute $15,000 to the project. So far as I know this was the first substantial contribution of the company to the University. Without Ray's interest and his introduction it would not have happened.

The warm friendship between the Ritchies and the Replogles continued and Ray came on our board of trustees. In the meantime, however, a tragedy occurred. At one of our annual pre-Christmas open house celebrations Edith Replogle was standing happily admiring the decorations in the living room when she suddenly collapsed and within a few minutes had passed away. The house was full of people, most of whom did not know the worst, but supposed that she was being taken to a hospital in an unconscious state. It was one of the most difficult parties my wife has ever experienced, for we had to carry on since dozens of other couples were yet to arrive. When the last couple had said their

124

goodbyes, then Josephine let go the flood of tears for her departed friend.

Since Edith's death Ray's generosity has been expressed personally in a substantial gift to the library project as a memorial to her. He is the kind of practical businessman, conservative in the best sense, who can appreciate the frustrations and headaches of the college president. And he can, with wry good humor and supporting encouragement, make a hard task much lighter.

One of my failings has been and perhaps will continue to be that I do not have the knack of mobilizing trustees to go after money themselves to the extent desirable for maximum productivity. I have tended all too often to assume the responsibility when at least a large share of it properly belongs to the trustees. And I am sure they would have assumed more of this responsibility had I been more aggressive in placing it on their shoulders. Perhaps I'll learn yet, but I doubt it. Mobilizing the trustees for fund-raising is a primary task of the college or university president. Often he does it in cooperation with his development director. But the president's part in this process is one of his most important fund-raising contributions.

In relating to alumni, my advice to young presidents is to ask and keep on asking everlastingly. Any alumnus who has any understanding whatever of the needs of higher education expects his college to ask for funds. He knows that if his college is not asking for funds it is not discharging its duty and is entirely out of step with American private higher education.

Of course, the president, in asking for funds, must interpret a worthwhile program and must make it clear to alumni that donations will produce a better college and hence a more valuable degree. Pleading with alumni to give to old Siwash to have a better athletic team or to finance a bigger and better alumni day parade is pretty well outmoded. Most serious minded alumni are more interested in the kind of educational product that is being produced and the relevance of their alma mater's program to modern needs.

Neither are alumni generally interested in the desperation, crisis appeals. Their response is more likely to partake of success psychology. If the college is developing a program, developing

125

adequate facilities, and attracting strong faculty, the alumni are more likely to give it not only their moral support but their hard cash as well.

At Pacific University alumni contributions in 1959 were minuscule. But with the advent of a full-time alumni secretary, an attractive alumni magazine, and the Program of the Sixties, alumni interest increased and waxed vigorous to the point that in 1965-66 the percentage of givers had exceeded the national average.

Systematic involvement which in fund-raising means systematic annual giving can be organized among alumni if the responsible administrator does a good job. Once developed, the habit of alumni giving tends to hold and it can be built upon as the alumni body of the institution increases in size and importance.

One of the most effective techniques our alumni office has used is the telethon. It is a method in which a friendly company is enlisted to provide its telephones at nighttime when they are not in use for the purpose of communicating with alumni. This has been done in Portland, Oregon, in Seattle, Washington, and in the San Francisco area. The alumni director develops a team of volunteer alumni who usually have a nice dinner together and then man the telephones in various categories, always trying to have the caller have college generation identification with the person called. Even though the individual alumnus gives nothing, he has a personal contact with the university. Even though he wants to complain, the door is opened for the repair of whatever estrangement exists.

Certainly it is true that there has been a minimum of foundation and government agency recognition of the smaller college and university, whatever the reason.

As indicated in Chapter VI, I am not convinced that this condition has been altogether the fault of the foundations or the government agencies. I believe that to a very large degree it has been the lack of initiative on the part of the smaller colleges and universities, particularly the church-related ones. I believe that leadership—and certainly this includes the presidents—has not been imaginative, resourceful and energetic in this connection.

126

Rather it has tended to be apathetic, defensive and sometimes resentful.

At Pacific University until just recently a grant from a private foundation or government agency was a rare event. This condition has begun to change. The change has been the result of imaginative, unselfish and energetic work on the part of certain administrators, professors, trustees and friends of the university.

It is my feeling that grants pertinent to departments or special emphases that have an academic base should be initiated by the professors in these departments. All too often we have given professors in small colleges a sort of soothing syrup and said to them in effect: "Since you're good teachers you don't have to worry about anything else, neither lecturing nor writing nor attracting foundation grants through research nor other extra class activities." Though I am a life-long advocate of teaching as the principal function of the professor, lecturing, writing and research are helpful corollaries of teaching and frequently the best professor also is active in this regard and vice versa.

A good example of the role of the professor in securing grants is the current step to develop an Education-Communications Center at Pacific University. In large measure the original idea came from Dr. Fred Scheller, a professor in the Speech Department, with a Ph.D. in the field of communications. The idea of developing a center in which all of our audiovisual aids would be brought together and in which every resource possible would be provided for the faculty and the students enlisted my enthusiastic support. In addition the excellent notion developed that the campus radio station would be transferred to the center and a closed circuit television and other such developments would be introduced.

Out of our discussions grew a request to the King Broadcasting Co., of which Mrs. A. Scott Bullitt, a trustee, is board chairman. This company had just built a new radio-TV center in Portland and had extremely valuable surplus equipment incident to moving from the old quarters to the new. Subsequently and largely through Professor Scheller's initiative, with my participation and support, the University received a gift from KGW Radio-TV of equipment valued at approximately $60,000.

127

In the meantime we sought help from the Hill Family Foundation, with the ideas being developed in the Speech Department by Professor A. C. Hingston and Professor Scheller and the formal application being processed by P. A. McLennan, who had just come on our staff as assistant to the president for development. George Geist, one of our trustees, was helpful in enabling us to learn to know better David Mason, the Northwest representative of the Foundation. Mr. Mason gave us a good hearing, visited the campus, carefully looked over the old Carnegie library which would be devoted to this purpose when vacated upon completion of the new Harvey W. Scott Memorial Library. We conferred with Dr. A. A. Heckman, director of the foundation, in Portland and laid a tentative written request before him. He then made additional suggestions for the final application. The result was an initial $61,000 grant to make studies and to prepare the way for a maximum functioning of such a center!

During the approach we stressed the fact that ours would be the only private college in our entire area that would have this particular kind of communications emphasis. It seems to me that this approach has not been properly exploited by smaller colleges. Too often they ask for support rather than developing something that is unique. Often the activity may not be unique, but the fact that it can be established in a smaller liberal arts college is unique. This is often extremely appealing to the men and women who sit on the board of directors of foundations.

In our years at Hartwick, although most of the major contributions came from individuals, money from small upstate New York foundations was of an extremely important nature. The White Foundation in Cooperstown made two substantial grants to enlarge the library facilities. The Clark Foundation provided annual support for our Nursing Department and extensive scholarships for students interested in this area.

One of the major foundations on the West Coast is Crown Zellerbach Foundation. As has been mentioned, we have fortunately become a steady and fairly substantial beneficiary of this foundation. I was most encouraged to learn that the foundation is extremely interested in the smaller college and has had many smaller colleges on its list for a number of years. I have had long conferences with R. G. Shephard, president, G. E. McKenna, treasurer, and with Charles E. Stine, secretary. The foundation is not interested in bricks and mortar directly, but is tremendously interested in helping the smaller, traditional colleges to cope adequately with the great problems of education today and being thoroughly modern and also basically sound. Mr. Shephard encouraged me to submit to them a number of ideas in very brief form so that if they attract the interest of the members of the board then they could be expanded as may be required. He advised against a thick, extensively detailed documented application in the first contact.

Too frequently the smaller colleges do not emphasize the importance of some kind of personal relationship, some kind of identification with the foundation. Although it is obvious that this direct contact cannot be managed in the case of many of the great foundations, at the same time there are hundreds of smaller foundations that respond positively to the opportunity to "come and see." In many cases they are vitally interested in a real opportunity to analyze the program of the institution and see what is distinctive and significant about it.

One of the foundations in Oregon which has been enormously helpful to small colleges, notably Willamette University, is the Collins Foundation. The Collins family have been prominent Methodists and have taken seriously the matter of stewardship of a great fortune. In our own case we could not expect, in view of the prior interests and commitments of the foundation, to receive a large grant but on our library project we approached the foundation, found the response most cordial, and received a grant of $15,000. Here again, sometimes it is assumed that a foundation or even an individual is wholly wrapped up in one college. Most foundations and certainly most intelligent individuals realize that in a given area it is important to have interests broader than any individual institution. The day of the one-donor institution is pretty well passed. The trend has been in the direction of supporting an idea represented by perhaps a cluster of institutions rather than concentrating all concern upon an individual institution.

Earlier in this book I have said that resistance on the part of church-related colleges to government financing had greatly diminished and would certainly disappear for all practical purposes. Nearly all of the private colleges I am acquainted with have gladly received government loans and government grants. To my knowledge no obnoxious government control has been claimed by any college president I know. At Pacific we have had fairly extensive loans and grants for buildings and for student aid. To date the government officials have been extremely cooperative and helpful.

The college I serve now has but little regular support from the United Church. This has been true of nearly all colleges which have come out of the Congregational tradition. Those which developed in the Evangelical and Reformed tradition have had better support. The United Church is, of course, a merger of the Congregational Christian Churches and the E & R Church.

Not long after I came to Pacific, I went to New York City and laid before the proper church authorities a request for assistance to "seed" our Program of the Sixties. At least in recent decades the record showed no substantial contribution to Pacific University. Yet, after a visit to the campus by Dr. Wesley Hotchkiss, director of the United Church Board of Homeland Ministries, and after filing a well-prepared and documented application, Pacific University received a grant in the amount of $100,000. This money was crucial as "seed" money. In large measure from it has sprung the whole impetus of the Program of the Sixties.

My earlier experience at Hartwick College from 1953 to 1959 was different. The college, though in a non-Lutheran community and populated mostly by non-Lutherans as students and faculty, was officially related to the United Lutheran Church in America and to the Synod of New York and New England. In the chapter on "The Financial Wilderness" I have described our appeal to the church for an increase of annual support to long-range financing to rescue Hartwick from a serious crisis. The church responded. While I was at Hartwick the annual support increased from less than $30,000 to $60,000. Of course, as the budget for the college burgeoned, the church support did not keep pace and proportionately decreased. Nonetheless, there was steady annual support, with its inevitable and concomitant price attached. It might be called college-church politics. Each year it was necessary to appear before the synodical board of education and plead the case of the college for added support and it was necessary to cultivate friends within the church in this direction.

Sometimes certain church leaders were not friendly. I shall never forget one occasion on which I arrived late for the synodical meeting in New York City at one of the great churches there. Just as I arrived someone whispered to me that one of the ministers had made a vociferous attack upon the college and at least by inference upon the president because we were not Lutheran enough. Apparently my activities in the National Conference of Christians and Jews and my speaking in many kinds of religious houses in upstate New York, including Jewish synagogues, was not heartily approved by this individual. However, some of my faithful trustees were there to defend staunchly our college and its president.

The above interesting action had occurred just before I arrived, but happily I was present at the time the college budget support came up for discussion. One of the younger ministers, an enthusiast for our point of view, rose and moved that support for the college be increased by $15,000. It was voted by a large majority. I could have cheered. Especially since I had not requested the $15,000 in the first place! It was a bonus for the college, collected because of a negative attack from a narrow-minded quarter of the church.

Another occasion for church politics is firmly fixed in my memory. I went to the meeting of the synodical board of education prepared to ask for an additional $10,000 support for Hartwick College. Imagine my consternation when the president of Wagner College, the other institution supported by the Synod, asked that the support of Wagner be increased substantially more than support for Hartwick. The result was a vigorous debate on the merits of bigness and smallness. At that time Hartwick was scarcely half the size of Wagner.

The issue was really not decided at the meeting and broke open in full force at the meeting of the synod later on. It happened that it was the last meeting I attended before leaving Hartwick to come to Pacific. I was prepared to speak long and earnestly if necessary, but took the precaution to distribute the

131

responsibilities and had members of the board to speak on our behalf as well as adding my remarks in the course of the discussion. There were volunteers for our cause from outside the board as well. As a result, on that occasion we administered a defeat to Wagner in terms of church politics. The two colleges were retained on an equal basis of their annual support. As I recall it, it was then that we reached the $60,000 annual support point.

At Pacific, since church support of any substantial amount has not thus far come from the conferences and at the present at least there is no general annual support from the national church body, there has been really no occasion to engage in this kind of maneuvering relationship. I welcome the freedom, but I certainly do miss the support, and I feel that one of the great weaknesses in the program of higher education related to the United Church is that there is no really aggressive effort to provide financial support for colleges related to the United Church. I do not believe that the absence of control should mean absence of support. We do receive some very slight support from individual churches in the West. We have hopes of increasing support but have not as yet been able to realize these aims.

Churches which sponsor or relate to colleges and endow them with a certain identification should face up to the problem of the survival of such colleges as first rate institutions. Many church-related colleges have come to the point of severing their ties or at least loosening them. The reason is all too clear.

One day at the Rotary Club in Oneonta a friend hailed me heartily and said, "Mike, I saw you helping a certain elderly lady across the street yesterday. Were you by any chance counting her pulse as you held her arm?"

Of course, the Rotarians standing around burst into a roar of laughter. They really couldn't conceive of my helping an elderly lady across the street as a matter of gallantry, as a Boy Scout act, or as a matter of genuinely friendly concern. They could only think of me in the role of a seeker of shekels for the little college on the Hill.

At Hartwick in those years from 1953 to 1959 I helped a great many elderly ladies and gentlemen across the street and up the steps at the college. And these activities did pay off—in money for the college, in new friendships, in increased respect for the dedication of many wonderful and philanthropic people, and in many humorous and otherwise soul-satisfying experiences. I think the unsung heroes in higher education are those who invest in these institutions to make them secure and to make them significant. Presidents and deans are important. The professors who do special research or who make themselves beloved by great teaching are important. But none of these people would be on the campuses unless some committed soul with money had decided to invest in the bricks and mortar, the equipment, and the salaries to put them there and maintain them in their work.

Mrs. James A. Dewar, who lived modestly on Ford Avenue in Oneonta but possessed a sizable fortune in IBM stock, was such a person. By the time I left Hartwick College in 1959 to come to Pacific University she had given or the Dewar Foundation had given on her behalf approximately a million dollars, if not more. I understand that she has continued to be very generous to the college in the decade since we moved away.

Mrs. Dewar had an all too rare sense of stewardship and dedication about her fortune. It was obvious that she felt herself to be a trustee of this blessing and that she was responsible to put it to good use for her community and for mankind.

I recall that this modest, quiet, great woman had three major philanthropies: The church, Fox Hospital in Oneonta, and Hartwick College. A fourth, if I am not mistaken, came into being while I was in Oneonta: The Salvation Army. I remember that she helped finance the education of the local Salvation Army leader in classes in Sociology at Hartwick College. It may be that she had contributed previously, but certainly she gained a new appreciation of the work of the Salvation Army through this relatively small but tremendously important piece of philanthropy. I understand that her interest has continued.

Of course, I visited with Mrs. Dewar many times and have innumerable reasons to be grateful to her not only on behalf of the college, but on our personal behalf. I remember one visit to her house emphasized by her humility and her democratic spirit. She had called me on the telephone and asked that I drop by the house on the way home after work. I arrived at her house thinking perhaps she had some comment to make about one of the scholarships she was giving. Instead she handed me an envelope and said, "Here's something for the School of Nursing endowment." I opened the envelope and found IBM stock certificates amounting to $50,000. Of course, I tried to thank her, but she stopped me short and said: "Gus bought IBM stock for little or nothing in the old days. It now has multiplied into a fortune without any great effort on my part. I must do with it some good, just as Gus would have done." Of course, Gus was Mrs. Dewar's late husband. I went on my way with a heart full of gratitude that there were such people in the world.

When needs of a dire and crucial nature would arise at the college I would make a listing, develop a careful and factual explanation which Mrs. Dewar always expected, and go to see her. One day I went down and explained that we wanted to build an extensive addition, more than doubling the capacity of Dewar Hall, a building she had donated and which was completed during my first year at Hartwick. She listened attentively to all the facts relating to the swelling enrollment and the need for this facility. She wanted to know relevant details about any project and listened with great intelligence. After I had finished describing the need for the new facility, she said: "Well, we'll have to ask Nathan Pendleton to see what kind of funds we have in the foundation."

Later we conferred about the matter and she invited me to a meeting of the foundation officers. I took with me the prospective builder. We discussed the plans and the costs and satisfied everybody's concern. Then the builder and I prepared to go, but Mrs. Dewar said mildly, "That won't be necessary, we'll just take the vote while you are here." And so they did, to give the college $250,000 for the new building.

Never did Mrs. Dewar make demands upon the college. Never did she say, "because I give you money, you must do things my way." That is with the exception that she wanted quality buildings which were to bear her name. And Dewar Hall, dormitory for women, was unmistakably one. Her other philanthropies while I was there included scholarship endowments and direct contributions in money. But perhaps in the last analysis an even greater contribution was the example she set for donors and for all of us who deal with the matter of philanthropy in the interest of higher education.

As I have said earlier, some of the narrow-minded ministers in the Lutheran Synod of New York and New England did not take kindly to my associating so freely with Catholics, Jews and persons of varying backgrounds. Neither did they like my inviting people of many viewpoints to lecture at the college nor were they delighted with the fact that we welcomed most eagerly Catholic and Jewish youngsters as students and did not make a superhuman effort to make sure that a majority of our students were Lutheran. In fact, only a very small percentage were Lutheran, that denomination ranking third or fourth in representation of the student body most of the time. Usually Methodists and Catholics led the way.

These same critics suffered a supreme shock when Miss Marion Yager died in Florence, Italy, and left an estate of approximately $2,000,000 to Hartwick College. Miss Yager was Roman Catholic. I do remember that some of these same ministers did have the grace to congratulate us on this good fortune and in some cases gave me lavish credit for bringing this money in because of my interfaith interests and activities. Apparently the "almighty buck" stimulated their appreciation for a liberal approach. Actually, I deserved no credit whatsoever on this score. Miss Yager left the fortune to Hartwick College in memory of her brother who was a devout Presbyterian while his sister was a Roman Catholic. Why she embraced the faith I don't know, but I do know that she had a great appreciation for the historic culture of Italy which is an outgrowth of Roman Catholicism in many respects.

Miss Yager was a "character." I shall never forget my first meeting with her. Dr. Arthur Seybolt, her lawyer and a trustee of Hartwick, took me to see her. I was nervous about the visit for I had been told that she was peculiar and crotchety.

As we approached her door I noticed a small table in the hallway, almost an exact duplicate of one of the antique tables in our own house. Then when I met the bright-eyed, erect but aged lady I jokingly told her that I fully expected to tuck the table under my arm and take it with me when I left. She was delighted

135

to find me interested in antiques and launched into an extensive discussion about them. All I needed to do was to ask leading questions. In fact, I went away in the prime position of being her favorite conversationalist.

On another occasion Dr. and Mrs. Seybolt invited Josephine and me to dinner with Miss Yager. She was then over eighty. After dinner she called for a special liqueur, the name of which I don't recall. Despite the church-related character of Hartwick I managed to join her with enthusiasm. Then, she picked up a case of long European cigarettes and offered them around. The ladies were non-smokers, Dr. Seybolt because of health could not smoke, and I had sworn off cigarettes (two packs a day) about two weeks before. However, with an apologetic thought cast in the direction of my doctor, I accepted the long cigarette and the dear lady and I puffed away.

So far as I know we never discussed to any great extent the fact that she was Roman Catholic. Undoubtedly she knew my broad understanding and appreciation of different religious groups, but certainly there was no aggressive cultivation along this line on my part. And certainly smoking European cigarettes and drinking a thimbleful of after-dinner liqueur did not bring Hartwick the two million dollar bequest. Doubtless, all these things may have helped and they do remain a delightful memory. Also, the correspondence that took place from time to time between Oneonta and Florence, Italy.

When her bequest was revealed after her death in Florence, I was flabbergasted at the amount. I had expected it to be perhaps one or two hundred thousand dollars. Dr. Seybolt, who in the meantime had died, had very wisely refrained from telling me the full amount of the fortune involved. The knowledge would undoubtedly have destroyed the ease with which I related to Miss Yager. Dr. Seybolt was wise in this and in many other things. I remember him as well as Marion Yager with great affection and thankfulness.

Another donor of Hartwick days, who is still my good friend, is Dr. Harry C. France of New York City. I first learned of him as a native of the Cobleskill area just northeast of Oneonta and was somewhat awed by the fact that he had become a famous financial adviser and the author of a weekly column in some 150 newspapers. The column advises on investments and Harry is a paragon of knowledge in this field.

I analyzed what I learned of Dr. France and figured that the approach ought to be in terms of his identity with the country of beautiful hills and low mountains in upstate New York where he grew up before he went to Wesleyan University in Middletown, Connecticut. I assumed he would still have a soft spot in his heart for this country and the institution serving it.

The hunch was correct, for twenty minutes after I met Harry France he was telling me with great satisfaction how he "sold skunk hides" in Schoharie County to get the money to help finance his education at Wesleyan University.

He willingly accepted invitations to lecture at Hartwick College, got acquainted with our program and our problems, and became a generous donor and a warm friend of both the college and of the Ritchies. Since that time I have spent many happy hours with him and his remarkable wife who at the age of approximately seventy years wrote a best selling book on how to raise babies. She had for many years been an authority on children and at one time was supervisor of nursing education for the Metropolitan Life Insurance Company. It was my great privilege to confer the Doctor of Letters degree upon Harry France, author of a number of books as well as his famous column.

Fred P. Murphy, for many years president and later chairman of the board of the Grolier Society of America, was another native of Schoharie County in upstate New York whom I learned to know. The same principle of identification was emphasized in our relationship. Fred, interestingly enough, is a Roman Catholic. But this did not keep him from having a deep interest in the Protestant college which served the area where he grew up. He has a lovely country place near Stamford, N.Y., and had been a financial godfather to Stamford in developing substantial industrial interests in the community, part of which consisted of factories for the making of bookracks to hold the famous encyclopedia published by the Grolier Society.

Fred Murphy became a deeply interested friend of Hartwick College, contributing his money and wisdom to its support and development. I continue to have a cordial contact with him through correspondence. Incidentally, I came to know both of the men just discussed through Dr. H. Claude Hardy who worked with me on such matters while I was president of Hartwick and who is now Professor Emeritus of Sociology and one of the great spirits in the community.

Sometimes an almost chance contact will trigger a gift. The gift in turn may trigger a series of relationships that result in substantial donations. One day at Hartwick I received a hand-written letter from a Miss Bernice Saxton enclosing a check for I believe $2,500. She stated she had heard a radio program in which some of our students told how they worked their way through college. She was very much moved and felt we should have this money to assist in the student aid program. I immediately checked with Dr. Hardy who knew Miss Saxton, but did not know of her reaction to the radio program. Then he and I went together to see her. She lived in a very modest little home where she received us quietly, but most courteously.

In the course of the conversation, after thanking her for her gift, I gingerly approached the matter of whether she was giving the $2,500 as a donation for that particular year to be followed by others, or whether it was all we might expect. She smiled and said, "Well, if IBM continues to prosper I hope to be able to do as much each year." What a pleasant surprise! And I understand Miss Saxton has continued to be generous to the college.

Luckily, the Northeast does not have all the generous donors. Here in the West perhaps the tradition of individual giving to institutions has not become as firmly rooted as is the case in the Northeast, but there are many persons who remind us of the generous donors of the Hartwick years.

One such is Miss Helen Green of Portland. She had been making relatively small contributions to the University for some years, perhaps as a result of her deep dedication to higher education and her membership in the First Congregational Church in Portland. When our library effort began I visited Miss Green along with Jack Pugh, the associate chairman of the library effort. We explained our needs to her and the importance of getting some fairly substantial gifts in order to encourage others.

138

She sat in her neat but relatively small living room and listened attentively. I handed her a subscription card, expecting her to want several days to think it over. She said, "I need to read this and think about it," and turned aside. One of us remarked that we would be glad to leave it with her, but she quickly replied, "Oh, that's not necessary, here's what I think I can give." She handed us back the card with the donation space filled in at $5,000.

Since that time Miss Green has continued generous support of the University. She is another example of the unassuming person of means who gives to the great cause of higher education with no thought of special recognition or of special reward other than the satisfaction of knowing that she is investing in one of the most important enterprises our country has.

Another example of quiet, unassuming, dedicated individual giving in the West is Hall Templeton, member of the Board of Directors of the Boise Cascade Corporation and a member of the Board of Trustees at Lewis and Clark College. I learned to know Hall through mutual friends and mutual interests in civic life in the greater Portland area.

He is a truly remarkable man. He is an astute businessman, is well read and deeply interested in the "why" of human existence. A conversation with him is always stimulating to me.

Hall Templeton is a man of substantial means. He is unmarried. A tragic accident in his youth brought him what to most people would be an unbearable handicap. In the accident both legs were severed below the knees. But Hall travels all over the country on artificial feet and only a cane for special support. Further, he probably has rowed more miles in a single-man rowboat than anybody on the West Coast. He has rowboats in Washington, in the Bay area in California, and on the Willamette River. This physical recreation keeps him vigorous and is both mentally and physically stimulating.

I hesitated to approach Hall for Pacific University because of his deep interest in Lewis and Clark and his interest in Whitman College, which he attended. A mutual friend reassured me that Hall's interests should be and are broader than a single or even a pair of colleges and that he would certainly want to have a

139

part in the great development program at Pacific University, especially the library project. We therefore offered him the opportunity to participate.

The result of our visit was one of the most interesting donation letters I received. He pledged to give $25,000 on a certain schedule. Then he added what almost no donor adds, the proviso that should fate take him out of the picture the letter should be considered a contract with his estate for the payment of this pledge. Actually, he sent 1,000 shares of Boise Cascade stock long before he would need to have sent it and much to our mutual delight, the stock was sold for $27,296.33.

Mr. Templeton's interests not only include the colleges as institutions, but he has privately supported for many years the education of needy students of various ethnic backgrounds, many of whom have been from foreign lands in various colleges of Oregon. I am intimately acquainted with certain of these cases. At its recognition dinner in the winter of 1965, the National Conference of Christians and Jews, Oregon Region, made its Brotherhood Award to Hall Templeton for his private living out of the brotherhood ideal in many avenues of his life, but especially in regard to assisting young people of various hues and ethnic background to have a good education.

I could recite other wide-ranging experiences in the Oregon region, but the illustrations I have used from both college experiences have indicated that "going after the cash" is not just a routine chore for college presidents to be done under dire necessity. It can be a fascinating and enriching experience.

College presidents obviously should not be called upon to make every call upon every individual or every other source of funds for the institution. As I have said, the president who tries to do this will soon cease to be a statesman and will simply be a money grubber. The development office must handle the machinery and the development office and volunteers must certainly make calls but, frankly, I feel that the privilege of interpreting higher education to individuals such as those I have cited and to hundreds of others whom I have known over the years is something I would sorely miss. Nothing in my sixteen years as president of a smaller college has been more deeply satisfying.

140

CHAPTER VIII

The Heart of the Matter: The Students

Too often university professors pursue their research, perform their tasks as consultants to government or business—all very brilliantly—and forget or ignore their students. All too often presidents interpret their institutions to their various publics, devise plans for new buildings, and raise funds for exciting and sometimes world-shaking programs without taking time to know and to listen to students who are the center of the whole affair.

This should not happen in any institution, and especially it should not happen in the smaller college. Individual concern and a sense of community should be at the heart of the small campus. In fact, these qualities have been taken for granted for so long in the small college that only today in the face of academic mass production are we rediscovering their importance. We are also looking closely at our small colleges to see whether these qualities are really there.

Some small colleges have become increasingly exclusive in these days of high tuitions. Some cater to the highly intellectual students. Others cater to the students who have the money to pay the bill. Still others cater to students of a particular religious denomination. I believe intellectual, social, religious, or financial exclusiveness in the small institution makes for a warped and unhealthy education.

The small college should enroll the brilliant student. Many of these students will be original thinkers, will develop the new theories, and will stand on the frontiers of intellectual discovery.

But this same college should enroll the nonbrilliant, the steady, and the plodding students. Among these in later years may be found stalwarts in the community, members of the legislature, and certainly a sprinkling of trustees who will decide the fates of the very same colleges. On the campuses of the small college there should also be a third group of students. These are the lopsided ones who do brilliantly in some of the high school subjects and poorly in others and average out about a "C." They are the forgotten ones in higher education today, sometimes being refused admission to the better colleges, often unchallenged in their areas of special interest and special skill, often discouraged and cast aside. Yet these students deserve an opportunity for college attendance and deserve the special attention that may enable them to be highly significant leaders and contributors to society. Among this latter group may be potential for creative leadership that could outshine either of the other classifications in importance to society. The passionate, dedicated, untiring one or two-talent person may accomplish more than the person of many talents who is unwilling really to invest his talents and to risk them in the market place of life.

The small college should try to enroll a wide sampling of students as regards geography, culture, race, and religion. The college which enrolls only the students from its supporting church constituency is deliberately shortchanging them in terms of cultural exposure at a time when understanding of other people's background is of the utmost importance. At our small university we are proud of the fact that in a student body of approximately 1200 we normally have students from 35 to 40 states and from 12 to 20 foreign countries. Racially, in 1969, we have 121 Mongoloids, 63 Negroes, and the rest of the student body Caucasian. Many religions are represented, including Catholic, Protestant, and Jewish.

There is no better way to learn international relations than for the boy from Baker, Oregon, to have coffee with the boy from Pakistan, and perhaps be joined by a girl from South America and a girl from New York City. The small campus enables people of wide difference to have close contact as individuals. The kind of isolation of particular groups that often takes place on the big university campus need not happen on the small campus.

Within the last few years, innumerable stories have been written about student unrest, about students protesting the anonymity of the big campus, about changing moral values, about the impending death of the "in loco parentis" concept, about the desirability of students participating in a decision-making role in the governance of higher education, and about other innumerable aspects of campus life. Although I cannot generalize about higher institutions, I do believe that the smaller college needs to have guidelines, perhaps not so many detailed and restrictive rules as in past years, but guidelines that give students a sense of security as to what the university expects of them.

As a college administrator, I am not ready to eliminate the no-drinking rule nor the rule against use of dangerous drugs. The fact that these rules are successfully broken by some students does not make them unsound.

On the other hand, I am not in favor of rigidity as practiced on some small campuses. The freshman who comes to college from a home where drinking is entirely taboo and where experiences would not give him any alcoholic sophistication whatever may be the first victim of a drinking party on campus. Just a few drinks may put him under the table, whereas the boy from the alcoholically sophisticated home may be able to appear relatively sober after twice as many. Obviously, the first boy needs counseling, not expulsion from college. But to throw the door open, to countenance a wide-open traffic in liquor in the fraternities and the dormitories, in my opinion, would be a serious mistake.

As I have said, much has been published about student unrest. Several years ago I began casually collecting articles on the subject from a variety of sources and placing them in a folder. Soon they overran the folder, and the articles, now numbering in the hundreds, repose in a pasteboard box in my study closet. Reading such articles does not provide much comfort, for the variety of expressions of unrest is matched by the variety of proposed solutions.

Black students have made some of the demands for change and have staged some of the demonstrations on American campuses. One of the most dramatic of these confrontations occurred at Cornell University.

Often black student complaints deal with the absence of curricular emphasis on black contributions to the culture. Complaints in this regard are quite justified. In the curricula of most schools and colleges in the past one could learn very little about Negroes other than their living in urban or rural slums, working at menial tasks, and out of their misery creating the Negro spiritual in music.

But there is much more to the black heritage. Demands for Black Studies emphasis should not be necessary. School and college leaders should have recognized this need long ago.

Fortunately many colleges are introducing Black Studies courses. It is unfortunate that in many cases the development has come as a result of bitter confrontation between Negro student leaders and college administrative and faculty leaders.

Perhaps as a result of the extreme tension developing from unfulfilled need and perhaps as a result of a new sense of race identity, Negro student leaders have in some instances demanded control of the Black Studies program and that it be open to black students only. This kind of academic segregation is bad race relations and bad education. White students especially need to know more about the black heritage and the current and potential black contribution to the culture if they (the white students) are to relate with understanding to black people.

Pacific University, as already pointed out, has developed a heterogeneous campus, with a high percentage of non-whites. And this development began as policy quite a number of years ago. In addition Pacific has stressed the study of race relations in courses in its Department of Sociology and through its summer workshop in human relations established in 1960.

But even so the university recognized the need for further emphasis on Black Studies and has established such a program beginning in 1969. As indicated in a previous chapter this program was established in cooperation with interested student leaders and not because of any sort of demand. Student participation has been entirely constructive in the development of this program.

144

The legitimacy of many student demands for change in higher education has been obscured for the general public by the preoccupation of the press and television coverage with the ugly confrontations and the violent or near violent demonstrations which have occupied buildings, destroyed property, threatened individuals, made impossible demands and above all robbed the average student of his right to an education. Leaders in many of these extremist demonstrations have not been interested in constructive change; they have not been interested in the reform of higher education but in its destruction. And what is even more tragic, they have no program sound or otherwise with which to replace it.

Responsible student, faculty, administration, and trustee leaders must indeed be willing to listen to proposals and even to demands for change. But they must not and cannot allow a few extremists to bring to a standstill the operation of a campus, to threaten the safety of individuals, and to deny the rights of others to have the freedom to teach and to learn.

It is my belief that this generation of students is far more intellectual than my own generation in the early thirties. They are far more committed to a search for values. They may not be as respectful of set rules of conduct, but they are more concerned about problems of social significance. They are committed to a search for a better world to a far greater degree than we were. Many of our present students are activists in their inclination. They want to do something. Some have joined the Peace Corps; others have been involved in racial movements.

Though I respect the intentions of our students and their commitments, I am concerned that those of us who guide them should challenge them with the responsibility of studying in depth the problems with which they are dealing before they act. In addition, we must help them see that most of the dramatic marches or sit-downs or other kinds of demonstrations are not the cure, although they may focus attention upon the problem. We must somehow challenge the students with the relatively undramatic but vitally important long-term responsibility of community leadership in seeking permanent solutions to problems.

Part of the uniqueness of the smaller campus is that its ex-

145

pectations can be known to its students. I suggest that the standard of excellence in extracurricular activities should be just as high as the standard of excellence in academic work. If we pretend to educate on the small campus the "whole man," then our responsibility extends far beyond the classroom door.

Of course our expectations in extracurricular activities do not have much challenge if the student is allowed to deal only with trivialities. I can appreciate the call for participation on the part of students. I believe it is valid for students through their outstanding leaders to have a participating role in curriculum making and in important campus decisions. I do not think that their role should be that of final decision making in many areas. My reason is that they do not carry the responsibility, and they are not accountable to the trustees of the institution. The various deans and the president are accountable to the trustees. They have to live with their decisions in many cases for decades to come.

In our own University in the 1966-67 session, proposals were made by students for the establishment of what was nicknamed a "Staculation Committee." Its membership included administrators, faculty, and student leaders. One month the president of the University or his deputy presides and the next month the president of the student body. The committee provides a face-to-face communication that has been most salutary. Many incipient problems have been analyzed, understood, and ameliorated by this group in earnest session. Many far-reaching plans for changes at the University have been incubated and brought to a realization through this committee. Generally speaking, our students at least have made it clear that they want to be heard, they want to participate, but they do not want to usurp the responsibility of the faculty, administration, and the trustees in making final decisions. And I think they are right.

On the smaller campus, it seems to me, there is a very deep responsibility for providing counseling services. The small campus which is at all up-to-date will have competent people as dean of students and dean of women. Adequately trained psychological counselors should also be available. But of course guidance and personal concern should go much further than that on the small campus. Arrangements should be made so that the student has close contact with his professors and has opportunities for the casual, friendly guidance that is often the hallmark of the better small campus. At Pacific University in 1966, the dean of students worked out a guidance program which brought into play, on an organized basis, this kind of relationship for the freshmen. It has been most successful. Generally, our professors express a personal concern in students. The observation of student and professor in earnest conversation along the walkways of the campus is a matter of daily occurrence, and the same is true in the coffee shop of the University Center.

During our years at Hartwick College, I remember that Dr. Forrest W. Miller, head of the Department of Biology, not only guided his students very carefully while they were in college and assisted them in finding opportunities in graduate and professional schools, especially in Medicine, but also was a walking dictionary of their whereabouts and their success or failure as alumni. At Pacific University, a number of professors exhibit the same concern for their students and the same intimate knowledge of their whereabouts and their success five to ten years after they graduate.

Obviously, even on a small campus we don't supervise what a student eats for breakfast; and we don't hear his prayers at night when he goes to bed; but the number of incidents of remarkable personal concern that crowd in upon me as I write would fill a volume. I recall one incident in which my wife telephoned me that one of our favorite women students was ill and that I should come to the Infirmary. I did so, delaying my leaving the campus on a trip for perhaps an hour. It was interesting that in this young lady's infirmary room, within the space of two hours after she became ill, there were the college chaplain, the wife of the dean, the wife of the president, and the president.

More recently my wife and I sat in the home of the dean of admissions with two parents from California, hoping against hope that a dreaded telephone call would not interrupt the conversation. The reason was that in a nearby hospital the son of these loving parents was in a coma fighting the fight of life or death. Thank God the telephone call did not come, and within a month we entertained the parents at dinner the very day the boy was taken off the critical list. He had been in a serious automobile accident and had more injuries than I could recount, including head injuries that were feared to be fatal.

Not too long ago, a handsome, successful optometrist in the United States Health Service came to see me. He is Paul Owens, who received his Optometry degree in 1966. Paul and his sister Paulette came to Pacific together from Jacksonville, Florida. They were Negro students, from a highly segregated community, coming into a type of academic life not readily available to them in the Southeast. I took considerable interest in these two students and watched with great pleasure their growth and development. They repaid our concern for them by becoming highly successful students and as alumni are reflecting great credit upon the University.

Sometimes people ask why the smaller colleges have generally escaped episodes of violence and serious student disorders. I think the reason possibly lies in the close relationship between the administration, faculty and students. The feeling of alienation may be present, but it does not reach the proportions which occur on a large campus. The unruly group ordinarily would not become significant on a numerical basis. A protesting mob of 5,000 students on the Berkeley campus may be only a small percentage of the total enrolled, but it is a very large and dangerous instrument of unrest in and of itself. On a small campus such a group in the same proportion to the total student body would be of a more nearly manageable size. However, any reassuring statement which is made about student unrest has no guarantee attached to it. When a trustee asks me to predict concerning our campus, I always express great confidence, but I guarantee nothing.

We have had a number of disturbing student episodes both at Hartwick and Pacific. Earlier in this book I have described some of these. One of the disturbing situations on Oregon campuses barely passed us by. Gus Hall, secretary of the Communist Party in the United States, was visiting Oregon and speaking on some of the campuses, including the University of Oregon, Reed, and Lewis and Clark. At certain other colleges the president or other authorities had refused him permission to speak. The newspapers were full of disturbing questions regarding Mr. Hall's right or lack of right to speak. At the time he was in Oregon, he was under court indictment.

Strangely enough, our students did not get excited about the matter until very late in Mr. Hall's schedule; and when requests came to the dean of students office for referral to my office, I was in San Francisco. By the time I got back to be confronted with the matter, Mr. Hall had left Oregon. I was very grateful for his departure.

It would have been very difficult for me to have approved Gus Hall's appearance at Pacific University, for I consider him a paid propagandist for the Communist Party and not a person who would lend dignity to the University platform. Nonetheless, I would be perfectly willing to have the ambassador from Russia speak on our student platform; and I would be very happy indeed to have an authority on communism describe it to our students, provided we would have an opportunity to ask appropriate questions.

In discussions with other presidents, I found very interesting differences of opinion. With one president I had a heated discussion on the subject. His point of view was that the college could simply say that Mr. Hall or any other controversial figure was invited by the students, and therefore the college in general could be absolved from any responsibility. With this position I disagree. It seems to me that the college has to be responsible for the speakers who appear upon its platform. The college cannot shirk this responsibility by simply saying that the students have invited him. Certainly in the public mind the college is responsible.

I believe most firmly that a college is responsible to see that its students are exposed to differing points of view on great questions before the country and before society in general. The college that allows only speakers of the most conservative ilk or speakers who agree with its particular point of view on its platform is certainly shortchanging its students. Noted people of contrary views can be paired on the program and sometimes even brought together in a kind of a debate. Often a distinguished

149

visitor can have his views examined carefully by members of the faculty. This kind of exchange is healthy and demonstrates that many vital questions are viewed differently by highly intelligent and dedicated people. Obviously, the college should make it very clear that it, as an institution, does not necessarily endorse the views of those who appear upon the platform.

A few years ago at Pacific University we had an amusing but in some respects serious "coffee boycott." It was beautifully timed by the student leaders to occur on the day that Tom McCall, candidate for governor, would be on our campus. They cleverly maneuvered Tom before the TV cameras and had him drink coffee from an improvised boycott stand set up by the students in competition with the regular snack bar.

As expected, the boycott hit the front page of the *Oregonian*; and the students collected a lot of interesting publicity. As a matter of fact, because the young lady pictured on the front page of the *Oregonian* along with candidate McCall was so pretty, the University's publicity turned out to be very positive.

Actually, the "coffee boycott" was set up because of a student protest of the price of hamburgers and the price of seconds on coffee. A committee of students had visited Robert L. Wylie, the business manager, but had not come to an agreement. Mr. Wylie conferred with me, and I had suggested that the prices should be dropped to a compromise point between the current prices and those demanded by the students. It was expected that the students would return to Mr. Wylie's office shortly for further conferences. In fact, he was under the complete impression that they had promised to do so. In the meantime, however, the golden opportunity for a dramatic boycott appeared in the person of candidate McCall and it was staged.

Afterwards, I conferred with the president of the student body, and assured him that we had intended to decrease the price of hamburgers and the charge for extra coffee. But under the circumstances, I said I could not make any change whatsoever because doing so would be responding to methods of which I did not approve. Consequently, no change was made in the succeeding month. However, at Christmas time I had long conferences with the president of the student body, and he agreed that

150

the students were unwise in staging the boycott and that further conferences should have been held with the business manager and, if necessary, with me. This was the point I wanted to make. Accordingly, in February I issued instructions that the disputed prices in the coffee shop be lowered. This was quietly done, much to the approval of students and faculty members alike. During the remainder of the year, no repetition of such episodes took place; and the student government and the president's office got along well.

Relations with fraternities are often the cause of real controversy. It has always been my point of view that fraternities are responsible primarily to the university in matters of discipline and business integrity. At Hartwick College we had problems relating to both these matters. One fraternity would not set its financial house in order, and the situation was so bad that at one registration period I issued instructions that the president and treasurer would not be registered. When they received this notice from the registrar's office, they appeared in my office and signed the necessary papers to remedy the situation. After that we had no trouble with this particular fraternity.

Another fraternity refused to cooperate in respect to disciplinary matters and appealed to national headquarters. They were very much surprised when the representative of the national office visited the campus and fully agreed with the administration, admonishing the chapter leadership in no uncertain terms that they were out of line. In my experience, the national office of a fraternity usually will cooperate fully to see that chapters respect reasonable rules of conduct.

When fraternities will simply not cooperate under any circumstances, it seems to me the administration of the university has to take drastic steps. In the case of one fraternity at Pacific University, repeated action by the dean of students office did not get appropriate results, and the fraternity house was closed by order of the Dean of Students. Not only did the students protest, but also the alumni. One alumnus conferred with me while I was on a trip to California and protested vehemently. However, when I discussed the situation in some detail with him and raised the question of the responsibility of alumni to see that fraternities live up to their high standards rather than to defend them when they are off the track, he became very cooperative. Especially on the small campus fraternities cannot be a law unto themselves; they must be a part of the university community and must respect the policies of the institution.

By and large, fraternities are losing ground in proportion to the total number of students enrolled in American universities. General living conditions for students have improved. The challenge of intellectual activity has grown and the status of the intellectual leader rather than the social leader has risen. Many factors have combined to make being an "independent" entirely respectable and in some ways preferable to fraternity membership.

On the other hand, for many students a fraternity does have something to offer, and many fraternities strive with real earnestness to make a positive contribution. At Pacific University all fraternities and sororities are local, and all have their membership lists open to students of all races, religions, and ethnic backgrounds.

One of the most exciting things we have seen happen at Pacific University is a renaissance of student interest in cultural and general intellectual emphasis. In our early days we were aghast at the poor attendance at assemblies. Often, it would be extremely embarrassing to introduce a distinguished guest speaker to a group of fifty to one hundred students, despite the fact that attendance was required. On the entertainment side, students called for "popular" programs; and it was almost impossible to schedule programs of a more serious nature. Art shows were held only intermittently. There was no functioning Art Department. Theatrical productions were presented; but the emphasis was not strong, systematic, and well organized. My wife insisted that I go to every musical performance regardless of how I felt because attendance was so sparse that we must needs set an example.

In the decade which has followed, a great awakening has taken place. Now we have two full-time professors in art in one building that is almost wholly used for this purpose, exclusive of offices. New art exhibitions are presented each month with the local branch of the American Association of University Women presiding over refreshments. Whenever possible, the artist is pres-

152

ent. The openings are held on a Sunday afternoon and are well attended by students, faculty, and community people. When the school's Community Orchestra performs, the audience is sizeable; many times for musical events the auditorium is crowded; and for some cultural programs there is standing room only.

For plays these days, the little theatre is often packed to capacity. The Portland newspapers as well as radio and television have covered performances from time to time and devoted their columns to Pacific University's activities along this line.

One of the most exciting ventures in the theatre has been that of bringing to our campus artists-in-residence for a brief period of time. Karl Malden, the actor, has been here for two weeks or more, and Victor Thorley and his wife, Mary, have been here a similar period during two successive years. Also, William Whitman flew in from the East and took a leading role in one of our plays. These dedicated theatre people have contributed their services, and the only cost to the University has been hospitality. Obviously, the stimulus to students is considerable.

Another principle running through all of the extra-curricular cultural activities has been the involvement of the community as a part of such a project. Art shows include from time to time the work of local artists and students. Members of a cast of a play may include professors, students, and amateurs from the community. Some of the beautiful costumes made for various productions have been designed by a volunteer in the community, Mrs. Esther Morgan. A professional costumer could not do a better job. In the Pacific Community Orchestra about 75 per cent of the players are students and about 25 per cent are talented amateurs from the community. This kind of faculty-student-community participation has a cross-fertilizing effect and has helped make Pacific a cultural leaven in the community. Our small University performs this function as well as any in the country, I believe.

All of this did not come about at once. The idea that a university should be the cultural leaven of its community has long been one of my favorite themes; but it is, of course, not original with me. Much credit goes to the keen interest of my wife Josephine, who has persuaded, cajoled, and insisted that I should be sympathetic to the arts. Much credit goes to John Horns, who started almost from scratch in the art department and has done a great job. Theodore Sizer, the director of theatre, has a special genius for persuading diverse groups to work together harmoniously. His productions in the theatre have been amazing in their excellence as educational theatre. His emphasis on extensive participation is one of the secrets of success. Before him, much pioneer work in theatrical excellence was done by Warren Pickett, who had been an instructor in English and little theatre director at Hartwick. He has a talent for making something out of nothing, and at Hartwick converted a basement into an effective little theatre. He and his charming wife Becky came to Pacific in 1960 and remained here for a four-year period.

The Music School in its co-curricular emphasis has done an extraordinary job under the leadership of Dean Albert Shaw. He has worked closely with Ted Sizer and John Horns in the theatrical productions. Pacific University's band and choir tour the West Coast. The Community Orchestra led by Raphael Spiro is making a name for itself.

In retrospect it is almost unbelievable to consider the contrast between now and 1959. Some of the change has been through administrative encouragement; some of it has come through enlarged financial subsidies. A great deal of this success has grown out of the imaginative and dedicated leadership of persons mentioned and those who worked with them, but in large measure it reflects change in the interest of young people. It testifies to the fact that American youth are interested in participating in cultural activities. In addition, the community appetite along these lines has grown apace. This whole phenomenon as illustrated on our campus has been one of the most rewarding experiences of our years in college work.

Students today are enormously challenging. As I have said, they are much smarter than the students of my undergraduate days, they are more culturally oriented, and they are more dedicated to values. In my opinion, they are more confused but they have good reason to be, for the world is more confusing. Those of us who are their teachers and their elders must listen to them as they voice their concerns; we must try to understand them; we

154

must work with them; and we must guide them without destroying their initiative. We must identify insofar as is possible with their problems and their aspirations, but we must not try to be their age or to think exactly as they think, for we are of another generation, and the future is theirs, not ours. However, we do have special responsibility for the present, and although youth are very much a part of the present, their educational experiences in the present must prepare them to assume responsibility for the future with wisdom and faith.

CHAPTER IX

Strange Bedfellows: The Trustees and the Faculty

Historically the two major power centers in the American colleges and universities have been the trustees and the faculty. The latter has been largely responsible and mainly active in respect to curriculum and instruction. Whatever may be his complaint, the American college professor has been amazingly free in his instructional domain. On the other hand, the trustees have been powerful forces in general policymaking, in developmental planning and growth, and sometimes in operation. The function of a board of trustees providing a link between the college or university and its publics is in many respects uniquely American.

Despite their common sharing of substantial power in the operation of institutions of higher learning, the extent to which faculty and trustees have communicated has been relatively minor. Throughout the history of American education there has been much suspicion from time to time between the trustees who usually represent the so-called practical, professional, governmental and business life of the community and the faculty who are looked upon as impractical intellectuals. It therefore may seem a bit strange to discuss these two groups of participants in the same chapter. Yet there is logic to it, for though they may be strange bedfellows, they are certainly in the same bed.

First let us pay attention to the faculty, a group of people who have been described as "those who think otherwise." Certainly finding and keeping an outstanding faculty is perhaps the most difficult responsibility of the president and the deans. Besides, the president has the accompanying and sometimes prior responsibility of finding the money to pay them. The situation is very likely to get worse before it gets better.

There are those who think of the president in the modern college as a consensus getter, as a catalyst, as a kind of a continuing academic conciliator, and not as a leader looking ahead, planning ahead, and sometimes working ahead of his faculty. Someone has said that there are so many differences in the university that the only thing that really holds it together is a common plumbing system. I hesitate to compare the president to a plumbing system, but he does have the responsibility of holding the place together.

After a good many years in the presidency and more than a decade of that time at Pacific University, I am convinced that complete unanimity on any campus is only a dream and that the president who is only a referee between disputing parties and only an academic co-ordinator of doubtful truces is not what the times demand. I cannot speak for the large universities. It may be true, as indicated in Clark Kerr's book, that the new type of president required by the large universities "will be a coordinator rather than a creative leader . . . an expert executive, a tactful moderator . . ."[1] But I do not think that this description applies to the small, private college or university facing serious questions of survival. Certainly the small college president needs to co-ordinate; certainly he needs to be an expert executive; and certainly he needs to be a tactful moderator. But in my mind, he needs above all else to be a creative leader.

The modern president in the smaller private college or university should have a keen understanding of educational needs and educational processes. He should be a competent analyzer especially of the unmet needs in higher education. He must have an imaginative approach to ways in which his institution can fulfill these needs. He must be acquainted with change and its implications; he must recognize when change is progress and when it is not. He must be conservative enough to hold onto the

---

[1] Allan Nevins: *The State Universities and Democracy*, University of Illinois Press, 1962, Urbana, pp. 118-19 as quoted in Clark Kerr, *The Uses of the University*, Harvard, 1963, Cambridge.

sound values of the past in higher education and progressive enough to embrace new ideas that are constructive and significant for his institution and its constituency.

I think the president must accept the responsibility to lead, or he should not take the job. Tranquility and unanimity do not necessarily reflect leadership. Rather the president should keep the faculty stirring with ideas. He should constantly keep before them the challenge of what may yet be beyond them and beyond the college.

The president's creative leadership does not mean that his ideas are necessarily holy, nor that all ideas should originate from him. He should employ administrators and faculty members who are chock full of ideas, and he should not repress or discourage them. Unfortunately, he will have to say "no" many times; pragmatically, he will have to practice the "art of the possible." He should make a special point of seeing that the ideas of others are given recognition and that those who show leadership in this regard are rewarded instead of restricted.

The ideal would be for every faculty to have a rich variety of backgrounds—educational, cultural, regional, and personal. Faculty members should not all come from the same graduate school; they should not all practice the same teaching methods; they should not all have the same political ideas; they should not all go to the same church or have the same cultural tastes; and they should certainly not all be of the same national, cultural, and racial background. The president, subject to the board of trustees, is responsible for the hiring of the faculty even though the individuals are suggested by the division heads and the deans. He is in the decisive position respecting whether he will have a drab monotony in his faculty or a rich variety.

Obviously, the academic background of prospective faculty members is important. At Pacific University during my time we have made dramatic increases in the number of Ph.D.'s on the faculty, and now the proportion of Ph.D.'s in the total faculty is respectably high. But I feel very strongly that the door always should be open for hiring the non-Ph.D. who has what we might term an equivalency in background and achievements. I have often said it would seem a pity not to be able to hire Jesus

158

Christ or Saint Peter in the Religion Department simply because they did not receive doctors degrees from notable universities!!

The emphasis upon publishing as well as doctoral degrees as a primary consideration for hiring even in the smaller colleges has had many negative effects. Too often both the degrees and the publications have little to do with creative teaching. Too often the publications produced by Ph.D. candidates find a place on the library shelves and are read and studied by practically nobody. Frequently these studies are in-depth investigations of minute factors which would never be significantly involved in the teaching of undergraduates in a liberal arts college.

On the other hand, I believe that every college president should encourage his faculty members to publish ideas in one form or another so that their peers may react to and test the soundness of such ideas. The energetic faculty member who has ideas to express can find an opportunity in the pages of professional journals; he does not have to publish a book every time he has an idea. It is an excellent discipline for a professor to submit his work to the critical eyes of the editors of such journals.

Another way in which professors can get their ideas before their peers and the public is to engage in lecturing and appearing on the programs of professional organizations from time to time. Such activity is a good test of the soundness of their ideas and of their ability to articulate ideas in an understandable and persuasive way.

An effective way to encourage these activities is for the president himself to get published from time to time and to engage in serious lecturing on occasion. I have deliberately done this through the years of my presidencies, usually in the form of articles in professional or general magazines. Some of them may not have been very profound; some of them were based on speeches and were published in the proceedings of institutes or conferences before which I have spoken. Some of the magazines have limited distribution, and some of them have nation-wide distribution. One of the values of the president's doing this is that he has a ready answer for the professor who says he is "too busy." He cannot gainsay the fact that the president is probably even busier.

The question of research in the smaller college frequently comes up in any discussion of publication. Too often research and teaching are thought of as "either-or." I do not agree. It seems to me that in the smaller college or university, useful and creative research can be done by the professor. Furthermore, I believe there is no reason why college seniors cannot be involved in useful research that relates significantly to courses being studied. My firm opinion is that research and teaching should be interactive and that the one should stimulate the other. However, I realize that some teachers are more research-minded than others and that sometimes the most brilliant researcher is a boring teacher. Then again sometimes the most brilliant teachers may be poor researchers. But I reject the notion that it *has* to be one or the other.

The matter of degrees, publishing, and research often has a direct bearing on salaries. Some salary scales even have separate categories for various degrees at various levels. In some colleges the publication of a book is an absolute requirement for an advancement to a top professorial level. In others, continuing research is of similar importance.

I do not believe in specifically tying salary increments to any one of these items. I believe that the quality of the teaching insofar as it can be determined should be the central emphasis. Due consideration by the department head, the division head, the dean and the president should be given to the other factors. Certainly the department and division heads should know what the faculty members are doing in these regards, what degrees they have, where they got them, and to what extent they are continuing to grow in a scholarly and professional way. But tying down and objectifying every element of salary advancement seem to me to be unrealistic and uncreative. I believe the way should always be left open for merit rewards to faculty members as well as to administrative officers. I think the department heads and administrative officers who are not willing to make a judgment despite the element of subjectivity involved should resign.

Of course, there are rewards in teaching other than salary. One of these is the familiar sabbatical. From its name, it is evident that this type of leave occurs after a professor has been around for a while. At Pacific University, the sabbatical is offered only after the faculty member has obtained tenure. In my view the sabbatical should not be simply a glorified "vacation" but should be a time for serious study and cultural enrichment. At Pacific University we have tightened the requirements for sabbatical and have asked that those who are going on sabbaticals submit definite plans of study and be prepared for a full evening's report to interested faculty members when they return and this in addition to a written report.

Several years after I arrived at Pacific University, I realized that we frequently hire young men who have not quite finished their doctorates for very good reasons. In some cases they had married and had a couple of children and were therefore unable to devote full attention to the doctorate. Their opposite number, the young men who were either single or whose wives were childless, oftentimes were able to finish the degree and thus were hired by universities that could pay more than we could pay. I then proposed to the board of trustees that we create another program called a Leave-for-Study Program. The program would operate on the same basis as the sabbatical, full pay for one semester's leave and half pay for a two-semester leave. But the granting of the leave would be at the discretion of the president and he would be free to emphasize the completion of degrees. Since this program has been in operation, we have enabled several younger faculty to complete their degree work. Further, the program has been a great asset to us when we are negotiating for the hiring of young faculty.

The mere mention of the word "tenure" often causes controversial discussion. To many faculty members it is an holy term. To many trustees and in fact to many administrators, it is anathema. Although I frequently find myself defending tenure to its critics, I must say that I have often observed the insidious signs of professional "dry rot" appear shortly after the tenure status has been entered into. On the other hand, it has certainly been a protection to professors who might otherwise have been persecuted for political and social beliefs.

One of the perennial problems in any college is that of communication between the various groups. From time to time misunderstandings arise between the president's office and the faculty because of poor communications. Hence, every effort should be made to relate to the faculty through the deans and the division heads in order to avoid problems whenever possible. Usually in colleges there is a faculty senate or faculty council. In some of the smaller colleges the faculty council has representatives named by the president and other representatives elected by the faculty. This is the case at Pacific. A little different arrangement prevailed at Hartwick, but the function has tended to be much the same. Often the faculty council or the faculty senate operates as a welfare body for the faculty and represents to the administration the faculty point of view. In the instances where there are administrative representatives named by the president who function in a voting way on the council, the notion of a confrontation is avoided.

As already indicated I have made a practice of participating fully in Faculty Council affairs. At Hartwick I chaired the council. At Pacific the faculty council elects its own chairman. Of course the dean or provost of the university is always a member. But I make a special point to attend unless some emergency prevents my doing so. In the relatively intimate sessions of the faculty council, many problems are discussed and "nipped in the bud" before they can become serious. In this smaller group, the president and the faculty members can be frank and open in their discussion. Certainly they ought to be so that differences are aired and negative developments can be discovered before they become serious. I have considered participation in the faculty council the best means of communicating with the faculty.

Monthly faculty meetings are useful, but they tend to be more formalized; and they do not serve the same purposes as the faculty council. It has been said that faculty members individually are wonderful people; but then they come together in a faculty meeting, they are "just faculty members." In the faculty council sessions, the individual is more to the fore; the president can be more effective in riveting attention upon the whole university than in the faculty meeting. Further, questions can be analyzed at length, and possible solutions can be hammered out without hasty votes being taken.

Another important group on a large number of American campuses is the American Association of University Professors. At Hartwick College there was no chapter on our individual campus, but the AAUP chapter served both the Oneonta State University college campus and the Hartwick College campus. I really do not recall too many activities of the AAUP in Oneonta, and I was not particularly active. However, through the years since my professorial days I have continued my associate membership in AAUP. At Pacific I regularly pay my local dues and from time to time participate in the chapter meetings.

We have a very active Pacific University AAUP chapter, and it has made some positive contributions to our campus life. At times I find myself in disagreement with proposals of the chapter, but in general it has been a useful instrument of stimulating activities which most of the time are for the benefit of the faculty members and for the university as well. I have never sought to suppress or eliminate the activities of the Pacific AAUP chapter. For obvious reasons, at every opportunity I emphasize my own membership and identify with the chapter, but not with everything it does. Quite naturally I have found myself on the defensive about the AAUP chapter from time to time and have protected it from those who would otherwise attempt to eliminate this activity.

It seems to me that university presidents should always remember that the faculty and students are basically the most important groups in the life of the university. But at the same time, they could not function without the administration and apart from other supporting elements in the life of a university. Presidents need to respect faculty members and their opinions. But it is also the duty of the presidents to remind faculty members that they are not administrators and that they do not have the responsibility of administration.

I think it is unfortunate that some faculty members, having no experience in administration and having no responsibility for the possible effects of their suggestions, are nonetheless inclined to spend a large part of their time in concocting ideas on how the university should be administered. Sometimes these ideas are good, and administrators should be duly appreciative of them.

Yet they have a right and obligation to emphasize their responsibility in decision making, and they should draw the line at improper faculty interference with this function. Faculty and administration have their interactive roles. They should enrich each other; indeed, they should support each other. But at the extremes their roles are different, and they should not be confused.

Historically one of the serious problems in university life has been the lack of understanding between faculty and trustees. Too often faculty have thought trustees to be a group largely composed of overly moralistic ministers and hard-headed, but dull and wealthy businessmen. On the other hand, the trustees have often looked upon the faculty members as irreverent and impractical intellectuals taking advantage of a sheltered campus position to poison the minds of innocent American youth. Of course, this description of the "understanding gap" is extreme, but it serves to highlight what has been a thorny problem for presidents through the years.

Currently college professors are learning to understand businessmen better and vice versa because of employment as consultants. Professors no longer remain on the sheltered campus. Businessmen are learning that college faculty members by and large are not dangerous radicals, and that some of them are quite conservative, perhaps too much so. From this new acquaintance businessmen are emerging in the minds of college faculty as highly knowledgeable about the problems in higher education, tremendously interested and productively generous. Frequently faculty find to their astonishment that a business leader is better informed about the general problems of higher education than the faculty member himself who has been following his own specialty.

In the case of the ministers, the conflict has been greatly reduced and suspicion allayed by the fact that ministers no longer have the pre-eminent position on private college boards of trustees which they once held and also that ministers are becoming far more sophisticated about problems of young people than they used to be. The new morality is a matter of open discussion in the churches as well as in the colleges. Most ministers today are highly educated and very broad-minded people. They do not look upon the complicated problem of guiding youth in the old "Thou shalt" or "Thou shalt not" simplistic terms.

Show me a college which has the reputation of being strong, and I will show you a college that has a top-grade board of trustees. The two go together. A poorly chosen, unrepresentative and inactive board of trustees is a burden. But a well-chosen, representative, and functioning board of trustees is the strongest support factor an institution can have.

The board of trustees should represent the business and culture of the area in which the college exists. In some cases, however, the community of a college is a national community; and therefore, the trustees should represent the entire country. When I first came to Pacific, I was amazed that the board neglected to adequately represent the business and culture of the Northwest. In the last decade this has been corrected, relatively speaking, and the board has been greatly strengthened.

There is an old saying that a university trustee should give, get, or get out. No president would put it quite that way; but at the same time, I do not believe any person should accept a trusteeship unless he is willing to give his money, his skill, and his wisdom to the support of the institution. Preferably all three; all are needed. I consider it rank hypocrisy for a president to persuade any person to join the board of trustees and not frankly tell him the role he should play, including investing a substantial part of his treasure in the institution.

If trustees are representative of the business and culture of an area, obviously their contacts are important. They can open doors to wealth; they can open doors to skills. Often they can be invaluable through giving advice in their respective areas.

Oftentimes trustees are the forgotten leaders in education. All presidents are perhaps guilty from time to time of taking them for granted. They should be involved. For trustees to meet only once a year is simply not enough. If a trustee misses the meeting, he is out of touch for too long a time. Of course, it is true that sometimes the best trustees cannot attend each meeting. Oftentimes they may head committees in their particular sections of the country and be enormously helpful without a perfect

165

attendance at regular meetings. Our Pacific University Board of Trustees now meets three times each year.

Quite obviously the trustees perform a policy role. In many cases they own and operate the institution. This is true at Pacific University. In other cases they are agents of a church which may own the institution. Sometimes the church does not own the institution but is legally related to the institution in that it has the right to nominate a certain number of board members. In any case, trustees have a policy-making function rather than an operational function. Yet again sometimes their skills are such, especially in matters of finance and construction, that they come close to performing an operational function. In the academic area they tend to be more remote. Perhaps this is unwise. Usually the president and the dean have a serious job of education to see that the trustees are aware of the kind of academic influence the institution has. Certainly working with the trustees is one of the primary functions of the president.

Both colleges I have served have been blessed by very able and understanding trustees during my tenure. Earlier in this book I have referred to the late Dr. Morris Skinner, the great, liberal minister who was chairman of the board at Hartwick College. I also worked closely with Charles L. Ryder, vice chairman, during my years at Hartwick. He succeeded to the chairmanship on Dr. Skinner's death. Charles had a deep understanding of the problems we faced at Hartwick, and he had a remarkable appreciation for the role of the president. His encouragement and support were a great source of strength to me.

At Pacific University the chairman of the board, when I became President, was the Honorable George Rossman, Associate Justice of the Supreme Court of Oregon. He was a wise and good man whose devotion to private higher education was deep and abiding. The Rossman Scholarships are a memorial to his generosity and to his role as one of the great legal scholars of the country. Judge Rossman was succeeded in the chairmanship by Ronald M. McCreight in 1962. Ron is vice-president of Jantzen, Inc. He has been a remarkably perceptive and resourceful chairman of the board. I have especially appreciated the fact that I could sit down with Ron McCreight and "level" with him. The

166

give and take between us is frank and open; the mutual respect and affection are sources of sustaining strength to me in facing difficult problems.

Never once have any of my board chairmen or in fact any members of the board ever attempted to restrict my exercise of the utmost freedom in speaking or writing on controversial subjects. The trustees have never interfered with academic freedom in any way whatsoever. They have allowed the administration and the faculty of both institutions to experiment, to be active in community life, to run for public office, and in general to be a liberalizing influence in the community. They have usually not been concerned about the religious, racial, political, or social backgrounds of the faculty or administration. They have given the freedom that is so necessary if colleges are truly to search for knowledge wherever it can be found.

The trustees have willingly and effectively worked on ad hoc representative committees for the devising of long-range programs, for the searching out of new administrative leadership from time to time, for the revising of personnel policies and for the effecting of organization changes. Though the trustees have every respect for tradition and for practices standard in the better institutions, they belie the stereotype that would picture trustees as unyielding believers in the status quo.

Too often the trustees and their roles are not understood in the academic community. All too often they are a somewhat unknown quality and quantity. To students they are absentee landlords and overlords. To faculty they are visitors to the campus with a vague familiarity about them engaged in meetings that generally precede important announcements of one kind or another affecting salaries, tuition charges, and other such "bread and butter" matters.

At Pacific University we have brought trustees and faculty together from time to time in dinner meetings. This has been a most helpful experience and has tended to eliminate some of the strangeness and encouraged warmth, understanding and good faith. Under discussion as this is written is the possibility of an all-day workshop session with trustees and faculty participating.

There are those who would suggest that American universities follow the European plan of having the control vested only in the faculty. The opposition holds that the functions of the faculty are teaching and scholarship, that the general policy-making, the support, and the general university management are functions of the trustees and their representatives, the president and his assistants. In state universities the trustees are the vital link between the university and the taxpayers who support the institution. And in a private university they are the most important link between the university and its various supporting publics.

Many students of the subject feel that the American system of trusteeship has been a great democratic factor in relating colleges and universities to their constituency and in providing for our country the greatest availability of higher education in the world. I would agree with those who support the importance of the trusteeship, but I would suggest at the same time that too little has been done to provide a fruitful interrelationship between the trustees, the faculties, and the students of the institutions they serve. There need not be such a severe division and such inadequate communication. Without in any way threatening the authority and function of the trustees, opportunities for fruitful interaction can be devised. They would seem especially appropriate in these days when both the faculty and the students are demanding a "greater piece of the action."

CHAPTER X

Ideals and Realities in College Administration

One reason college presidents grow old before their time, die in office, retire early or simply get fed up and quit is that they are constantly torn between the ideals they seek to achieve and the realities of everyday campus operation. Sometimes the conflict is simply too much to take. Often the president handles the problem reasonably well but wears out long before the retirement age. Some hang on stubbornly but retire at sixty-five, defeated and broken.

An old and continuing conflict is the question of seeking to educate the whole person or just his mind. Should the institution be concerned about the social development of the student and his moral development or should it concentrate only upon the stimulation of his intellect? Well-rounded education has been the stock-in-trade of the small college for many generations, but all too often its academic standing is measured by the number of Woodrow Wilson Scholars or Rhodes Scholars who have graduated. All too frequently it is measured by the research of its professors rather than the amount of time they give to counseling the students as they try to develop personal as well as intellectual maturity.

When Dr. Frank Graham was president of the University of North Carolina and it was a relatively small institution, he is said to have turned the front porch light on one evening a week. This was a signal that he was at home to students. They came to see him to talk about ideas and books and other things. They knew him personally and he had an enormous and direct influence on generations of students in Chapel Hill.

Certainly a great many small college presidents today would like to have the time to turn the porch light on and signal the students to visit with them as did Frank Graham. But unhappily the complexities of the presidency in these days rule out any consistent policy and practice along these lines. The intimate, regular student discussion group with the president like the regular seminar and class he used to teach is mostly a myth today. Such activity continues as wishful thinking on the part of the president but is seldom a practical possibility.

Though much educational experimentation takes place in the small colleges, on most of our campuses it is severely limited by practical conditions. Funds are so scarce and constituencies are often so critical that the risk elements in many experimental programs are simply too great. All too often a spirited and highly imaginative young dean enters a presidency only to find his dreams impossible of fulfillment and his innovative programs consigned to the wastebasket. It may not be a matter of stubborn trustees or community barriers; it simply may be the harsh practicalities of today's crisis conditions in higher education.

There are few college presidents who lack sympathy for needy students. Frequently the presidents themselves worked their way from their freshman semester to their doctorates and have a deep appreciation of the rocky road of the student who is without family financial backing. But the small college today whose one thousand students must have full scholarships is headed for bankruptcy. Even to approach a balanced budget the small private college must have a reasonable proportion of its students from the more favored financial homes. Consequently the president finds himself constantly vetoing pleas from the admissions office for increased funds to provide financial aid for needy students and some of the case histories are appealing enough to prompt Midas himself to generosity.

Every small college president I know today is literally working night and day on some major bricks and mortar fund-raising project. In so many cases the president would really prefer raising funds for endowed professorships and for special programs to enhance the academic reputation and service of the institution. Yet the buildings are necessary, and often the funds are more readily available for buildings than for programs. This condition is not necessarily the result of dramatic student enrollment. At Pacific University, since the beginning of the decade, we have either constructed or have in the blueprint stage most of the key buildings on the campus. Every one of these buildings was needed—perhaps not in the same size—twenty years ago. Yet I would much prefer to seek support for significant programming than to "chase the bucks" for bricks and mortar.

Even in the use of many facilities the president is caught between what some people might think to be the ideal situation and the realities of need. Take the new university center on our campus for example. Should it be wholly reserved for students or should it be open to the service of the community which has no such facility? Incidentally, by making it available to the community, the community has the opportunity to share in some of the costs of operation. Fortunately in this case the very sound notion of the university as a community cultural and educational center can be invoked. In a small town there is great interrelationship with the campus. In our situation the public high school reciprocates in terms of facility use and the new city swimming pool is available for university rental. Yet I am constantly engaged in interpretation to answer the obvious questions.

The athletic program on the small college campus has been a subject of acrimonious debate for many a decade. Presidents are sometimes over-persuaded by the alumni and the community and allow the athletic tail to wag the academic dog. Almost invariably this situation becomes increasingly unhealthy as the years go by, and the president finds himself in an untenable situation.

The problem of expense is especially pressing on the small college campus. Actually small college athletics costs far more, relatively speaking, than does athletics on the large university campus. The small colleges in most cases do not have large ticket sales and do not allow outside groups to provide special funds for athletics. Hence, athletics must be financed out of regular university budgets and must be viewed as a part of the educational experience of the student. The question of "how much" money

171

can properly be spent upon intercollegiate athletics is a nagging one for every small college president I know.

In the old days when a majority of private colleges were closely held denominational institutions, religious emphasis was specifically defined and the president often either followed the clearly spelled out or emphatically inferred point of view of the church leaders—or he didn't last very long! Today presidents rejoice in the greater freedom even in the relatively conservative denominations. But the greater freedom has caused serious conflicts. Should the president eliminate compulsory chapel in the name of religious freedom? If so, what happens to attendance? In the cases with which I am acquainted, attendance falls off to almost nothing. And yet I feel strongly that chapel attendance should not be compulsory. Having said that, I must add that I have no solution to the problem.

Does religious freedom mean that there is no organized Christian emphasis on the campus which calls itself Christian? Assuredly I would be the first to say that performance is more important than profession and I would cite our own multi-racial and multi-religious student body as an example of our practice of Christian principles. I am very proud of our distinguished Department of Religion and the fact that professors approach the subject as scholars and not as stem-winding exhorters. But is the role of campus corporate worship to be lost? Can such worship be so arranged as to be inoffensive to any group and thus be appropriate for compulsory attendance? Or should there be Protestant, Catholic and Jewish Chapel? And if so, how about appropriate places for Moslems and Hindus?

If not in the form of corporate worship, how can the needs for religious expression, other than on Sunday morning, be satisfied? How does the president answer the critics who declare that the institution is not "Christian" unless it requires chapel and unless it requires a specific number of credits in religion? A forceful rejoinder is for the president to explain patiently that the institution is religious in practice, that courses in religion are voluntarily crowded and even that a good many students actually go to their own churches in town on Sunday morning. The whole subject is a source of considerable frustration for the president—

172

who nowadays is likely to be a layman—and who has at the same time a budget deficit to worry about, a faculty committee protesting that the teaching overload be met, and a meeting with the student body leaders to discuss student representation on key university committees scheduled for the following week.

Ideally the president of any college, large or small, is a person of scholarly aptitudes and of substantial capacity to think and plan. But in his hectic life today, the college president is hard put to it to find any time for uninterrupted concentrated thinking. Even when the president is lucky enough to have a free night at home in his study, he isn't guaranteed quietude, for there is always the telephone. And any college president's telephone is likely to be the busiest in town. But the calls do limit uninterrupted, concentrated thinking. All presidents need it. About the only way they can get it is to leave home.

One Eastern university is reported to maintain a country retreat for its president for this very reason. It is probably a good investment. In his book *Academic Procession*, Henry Wriston tells how he always maintained two offices, one as a sort of retreat for reading, writing and thinking. Dr. Wriston was the highly successful president of first Lawrence College, and later Brown University.[1] But on many of our campuses the clamor for office space is so loud that any such arrangement by the president would probably provoke a professorial revolution.

So most presidents steal what little time they can and address themselves to reading, writing and thinking in between other chores. I always carry a book in my attaché case when I am on a trip. Many thousands of feet above the earth in a jet I can really finish the chapter some expert has written on how a college should be run and I can think about it. Perhaps I may not be able to put all of his ideas into action when I come "down to earth" and return to my office in old Marsh, under the great oaks, on Pacific's campus. But the reading and the thinking certainly help immeasurably.

Presidents of the smaller private colleges and universities have for generations stressed the importance of small classes, but small

---

[1] Wriston, *op. cit.*, p. 30.

classes and sound economics in budget-making do not always go together. This is especially true in the college which has considerable student mortality after the first two years. In such a college the advanced classes are likely to be quite small anyway. Then if the college restricts beginning classes to fifteen or twenty, the student-faculty ratio is so low that even the highest tuition cannot possibly pay the faculty salaries. Unless the institution has an enormous endowment, it is sure to be plagued with deficits and to be threatened with eventual bankruptcy.

The same applies to the building of dormitories. Oftentimes college planners talk about the desirability of small groups of fifty in dormitories, but such an arrangement is a doubtful luxury in a college which is seeking to pay off the indebtedness of the dormitories with the income produced. How much more economical and budgetarily sensible is the dormitory of 200 students. All too often the ideal condition gives way to the fiscal realities with which the president and the business office are faced.

Sometimes enthusiastic faculty, alumni and friends of a university will urge establishment of a new program or construction of a new facility which appears highly desirable to the president. Perhaps it is the fulfillment of a long-held dream of many in the university community. But when the decision is made and the hard work begins, all too often enthusiasm cools.

Especially disappointing is the university friend who has applauded the new project and has told you what a remarkable leader you are, but who either is "completely committed" so far as his donations are concerned or contributes a "token" amount.

Fortunately this disillusioning experience is countered by other more encouraging responses. Example: The wealthy friend who surprises you by giving several times as much as you expect.

On occasion students shake your faith. They demand freedom and their demand is granted with the assumption that they have taken seriously the obligation to act responsibly. Your disappointment is great when in a given instance freedom is treated as license to create chaos. Fortunately the "batting average" on the part of students in this regard is better than commonly supposed.

The demand of black students on some campuses for segregated black studies courses, living quarters, and even recreation centers is disillusioning. It is especially so to those of us who have spent a great part of our professional life fighting for the right of the Negro to participate fully in the mainstream of American life. Fortunately the soundest and most respected Negro leaders still point in this direction.

Although I have rejected in other parts of this book the idea of "publish or perish" for faculty, I have also emphasized the importance of their taking every opportunity to put ideas before the jury of their peers in the profession. One way to do this is to publish.

Most books by academic people have small attraction for the commercial publishers because of their limited potential readership, but they are important to that readership and to the profession. Ideally every campus should have a university press to publish worthwhile books by the faculty. But for small colleges this is entirely impractical. There would seem to be a fruitful area here for cooperative action by smaller colleges. Establishment of a regional university press supported by small colleges would seem practical and certainly would be a great stimulus to scholarly activities by the faculties in such colleges.

I have sketched only a few of the perplexing and frustrating conflicts between what the president and the trustees of a small college would like to do and what they can do. To a large extent it is this ever present and severe conflict in the mind and heart of the college president which eats away his optimism and dims his hope and often leaves him beaten and embittered.

Yet despite the wear and tear of the conflicts I have described, and despite the fact that the smaller college is far from ideal, it does have special values and a special place today. The current disenchantment with the great university or the multiversity as it has come to be called emphasizes the point. The lack of communication on the mass-production campuses and the tragic sense of loneliness and the poignant need for identity have all been widely publicized. The rebels at Berkeley and the rebels on the Columbia campus, in part at least, were seeking a sense of community and were crying out for more than the identification of a number on a punch card. Among other things, they were protest-

175

ing shoddy teaching by young Ph.D. candidates while the distinguished professors they came to study under served well-paid consultantships off campus. They were calling for a new emphasis upon teaching as the center of campus emphasis at the undergraduate level. Whether these rebels knew it or not, they were protesting the absence of a real commitment to value-seeking and an emphasis upon something more than the intellectual.

Violent demonstrations have taken place all over the country and in universities of various sizes. A special result of the revolt against the multiversity is a kind of "rediscovery" of the small college in America. Thousands of students who lose themselves on the 10,000 to 25,000 student university campus with resultant disillusionment and dissatisfaction could find themselves and have a creative role on the 1,000 student campus. It is manifestly futile to expect individual emphasis and much of the sense of close community on an undergraduate, mass-production campus.

Such a point of view is underscored by the president of Cornell University in a series of addresses at Princeton University. In his address Dr. Perkins said: ". . . Those students who need the sense of security that comes from being a member of a smaller, tighter community should not come to the University."[2]

In a similar vein, Dr. Esther Rauschenbush, president of Sarah Lawrence College, urges that universities stop admitting undergraduates who are not ready for the less personal and more professional atmosphere of the graduate-school-dominated campus. She urges the establishment of many more small colleges so that students can experience "face-to-face" education.[3]

A great number of us have been saying this kind of thing for a long time. But not enough people have become "believers." They have accepted rather the "bigger and better" assumption. It is good to see the personal emphasis possible in the small college recognized by such leaders.

One of the most effective statements on the small college which did elicit respectful attention a number of years ago was that by Elton Trueblood, a former big university (Stanford)

---

[2] New York *Times*, Education Page, Nov. 7, 1965.
[3] New York *Times*, Education Page, Nov. 7, 1965.

professor who deliberately chose to teach on a small campus (Earlham). In a significant article published in the *Reader's Digest* and reprinted and distributed all over the country, Dr. Trueblood cited one of the key values of the small college in these words: ". . . every student has the opportunity to find and engage in those activities which will develop his maximum capacities."[4]

My own experience has included both the small college and the large university. I was graduated from a small college and took advanced studies in some of our larger universities. I was on the staff of a small college before World War II and, after military service, taught for nearly seven years in a large university.

I feel that many of the frustrations in the multiversity that have created, as the *Atlantic Monthly* puts it, the "troubled campus" in the United States are either not present or are minimized in the small college environment. In such an environment the student who is at all perceptive and responsive has an optimum opportunity to find a sense of direction. He has a better chance to develop a wholesome social maturity and there is no reason why he should be symbolized by an IBM card, despite the fact that some small colleges use IBM machinery to good account.

In most of our small colleges, many of them church-related, there is an institutional and, hopefully, student commitment to values basic to our American culture. Although students may sometimes complain about the rules and restrictions in many of our small colleges, these very guidelines indicate institutional concern for the individual and his development.

In the better small colleges there is much respect for significant research, but primary emphasis is upon good teaching. Promotions are not tied to the "publish or perish" rule or to research projects as the "Open Sesame" to the best campus job. Research which may be the "queen bee" in the multiversity is the "handmaiden" of good teaching in the small college.

Leaders in higher education have expressed new interest in the small college in the wake of the revolt against the "multiversity." Here is just a sampling of their comments:

---

[4] "Why I Chose A Small College," *Reader's Digest*, Sept., 1956 (reprint).

Paul Woodring, education editor of the *Saturday Review*: "I sympathize with the students, but they are naive if they think they can solve the problem of size by staging sit-down strikes or by demonstrating on campus or off. Those who want personal attention and the intimate environment of a smaller institution should leave Berkeley immediately and transfer to a small college."[5]

Earl J. McGrath, former U.S. Commissioner of Education, ". . . if I had a child of college age I would apply all the pressure I could within the modern doctrine of paternal non-interference to persuade him not too attend the large academic mass-production centers."[6]

Walter Youngquist, professor of geology, University of Oregon, ". . . in many fields, the small college can offer more than the big school. It can offer the chance for a boy or girl to be an individual, at a most formative time in their lives."[7]

Despite its obvious values, the small college is seriously threatened today. The principal threat is financial. Only aggressive efforts in development and assiduous public relations to bring its merits to the attention of its several publics will enable it to grow and prosper in a qualitative way. The stronger of the small colleges will survive. But the question is how will they survive— as institutions of doubtful quality, educating only the left-overs and the misfits or as institutions of first choice, as innovative leaders, and as the spark and stimulus of higher education?

In the face of these question marks many presidents of private colleges are quitting. Many are refusing when proffered the presidencies. I am frequently asked, "What can be done about it?" One effective answer is that "the same things that can and should be done about the presidents who are quitting in the state universities." They, too, are carrying impossible burdens. Some fundamental changes must be made.

It is necessary that even the smaller colleges will have to

[5] *Higher Education for All?* (Proceedings of the 27th Annual Pacific Northwest Conference on Higher Education), 1965, pp. 32-33.

[6] *College and University Business*, January, 1966, "Will the Independent Liberal Arts College Survive Present and Future Pressures?", p. 52.

[7] "Nobody Knows Me," Reprint, July, 1965, *North American Review*, p. 34.

provide executive vice-presidents or provosts to carry the principal day-to-day administrative responsibilities for campus operations. This will free the president for policy planning, for work with the trustees, for the enormously important task of interpretation of the college program, and for performing his role in securing the resources that will sustain the institution. The president who is so busy doing that he has no time for thinking is an all too familiar figure in higher education today. He is woefully the man in frantic motion. He must be given the kind of assistance that will remedy this condition. Whatever the cost, such an improvement will be the most productive investment the college could make.

Shortly after I came to Pacific University, I wrote an article entitled "I Am Glad to Be A College President." It was published in a national magazine. I wrote it largely because I was somewhat "fed up" with the complaints of college presidents who were resigning in large numbers and rationalizing their resignations in print. I deliberately emphasized the positive side of the presidency. Now after having been president in two institutions for a period of over sixteen years, I am asked the question, "Are you still glad?" The answer is emphatically, "Yes." As I said in the article, "I am not always happy, but I am glad." I am glad to have had these many years at the center of policy-making in two colleges and I am glad to have been a part of decisions that I believe were basic to their development into stronger, more significant institutions. I am glad to have been a part of the American academic community during the most exciting period in its history. If one can endure it, the presidency of a small college guarantees a liberal education. And, of course, it guarantees automatic membership in the Order of the Turtle.